The Wo

Sixty Five Roses

~ An insight into living with
Cystic Fibrosis ~

by Kairen Griffiths

Cover illustration by Emily Griffiths

First edition

© Kairen Griffiths 2020

ISBN: 978-1-71667-774-8

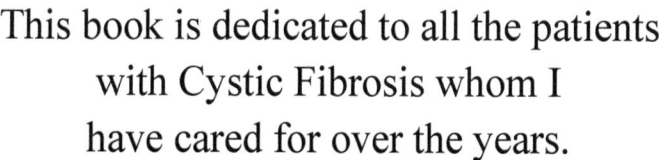

This book is dedicated to all the patients with Cystic Fibrosis whom I have cared for over the years.

The 65 Roses Story

The "65 Roses" story dates back to 1965 when an observant 4-year-old, hearing the name of his disease for the first time, pronounced cystic fibrosis as "65 Roses." Today, "65 Roses" is a term often used by young children with cystic fibrosis to pronounce the name of their disease.

65 Roses® is a registered trademark of the Cystic Fibrosis Foundation.

Disclaimer

This book is semi-autobiographical. Most of the characters in the book are based on patients whom I have known over the twenty-six years that I worked in the field of Cystic Fibrosis. Some of the stories told comprise a composite character, based upon several people. Others are true patient stories. All patients included in this book have given their express permission for their stories to be told. For those patients who have died, their families have generously given me their blessing to allow the experiences of their loved ones to be recounted in this book. I am truly grateful to them all and hope that I do justice to their incredible stories. Patient names and identities have been changed in order to protect confidentiality, except in two cases where I was specifically requested to use real names. I have also used the real names of some of the professional colleagues that I mention in the book as it would have been difficult to disguise their identities. Each of these colleagues are aware of this and have allowed me to do this.

All medical and clinical facts quoted in this book are believed to be correct at the time of printing.

Nothing in this book should be taken as an allegation against a real and living person or against a real institution. All untrue 'facts' herein that could be construed as allegations should be regarded as part of the fictional side of this book.

~ Introduction ~

Imagine the following scenario. You have recently given birth to a beautiful baby. Everyone is surrounding you with congratulatory messages and gifts full of happiness and delight. Your child is the apple of your eye, your new little bundle of joy who looks just perfect to you and to everybody else.

And then, the bombshell.

'Your baby has cystic fibrosis'.

Suddenly, your world is turned upside down. What does this mean? Am I dreaming? Tell me this is not happening. What do we do now? Will my baby die?

The shock and disbelief that must hit a new parent when they hear those words is unimaginable. Since the 2000's, all babies born in the UK are tested at birth for cystic fibrosis (CF). Many, many parents have heard these words since then and they will all have felt the same emotions.

Years ago, the outlook was bleak for those with CF - today, there is much hope and optimism for those with the condition, for those who look after people with it and for the health professionals and scientists involved in caring and treating patients. There is hope on the horizon, but for those living with CF every day of their lives, it remains a complicated and difficult condition to manage.

I have been carrying this book around in my head for a long time. How to write it, where to write it, who to include in it and will I do these people and their stories justice?

I have recently retired as a nurse, with forty years' experience, mainly in the NHS, and with twenty-six of those years working as a Cystic Fibrosis Nurse Specialist in a major teaching hospital in the North East of Scotland.

What a job it was. One that was full of the most incredible experiences, a chance to meet the most inspirational of people and such a roller coaster of a ride – from joyous to heart-rending.

CF is a complex and challenging condition; one that I will expand upon more fully in later chapters. It is an inherited, recessive disorder (meaning that both parents need to carry and pass on a copy of the faulty gene) and it currently affects around nearly eleven thousand people in the UK today.

I believe there is no other job quite like that of the Cystic Fibrosis Nurse Specialist - we get the chance to get to know patients and their families incredibly well and we accompany them through the best and worst of times. I had known some of the patients for twenty-six years when I came to retire and you really do become part of the family, whether you choose this or not. It is an extremely privileged position to be in; a chance to be a part of other people's lives when they are going through the most traumatic or uplifting of times. I have been to many weddings, twenty-first birthday parties and fundraising events, but I have also been to countless funerals and been alongside patients as they reach the end of their lives. This is a great privilege but it can also be an unbelievably tragic and poignant situation for all involved.

CF affects many of the body's major life systems. As a result of this, people with CF are cared for by a multitude of health professionals, collectively known as a multidisciplinary team. Multidisciplinary teams in NHS hospitals are now commonplace for a whole variety of diseases and illnesses, but people with CF were one of the first groups to be looked after in this way. Working within a multidisciplinary team can bring its own challenges but can also be very rewarding, especially when different disciplines work together, bringing their own expertise, ideas and respect for each other.

During my career in CF, I was also fortunate enough to work with nurses and other health professionals throughout the UK and further afield. I learnt so much from these other experts and I relished the opportunities to attend meetings and conferences all over Europe. To meet others from such diverse backgrounds but all with a common goal - to care for those with CF - has been without any doubt one of the highlights of my nursing career. I will never forget many of the CF colleagues and friends I have met over the last twenty-six years and consider myself very lucky to have been in this position.

This book is dedicated to my family, friends and work colleagues, all of whom have given me support and encouragement over the years - I am truly grateful to you all. But most of all, this book is dedicated to all the patients and families I have met; an amazing and inspirational group of people - you have all taught me so much about how to live life and enjoy every moment – a heartfelt thank you to you all.

1
~ What is Cystic Fibrosis? ~

Cystic fibrosis (CF) is the UK's most commonly inherited genetic recessive disorder. By this, I mean that both parents need to carry and pass on one copy of the faulty CF gene in order to have a baby with CF.

I once worked with a wise respiratory professor who described the faulty CF gene as being two letters that have been printed the wrong way around in one word of one page in a dictionary. All the other thousands of words in the dictionary have been printed correctly and on skimming through the book, no one would notice this misprint. But in fact, this one misprint can have a major and devastating effect on a person. This is CF; everything else can be working perfectly but due to this one small misprint, a person's life can be changed in an incredible way.

One in every twenty-five people in the general population in the UK will be a carrier of the CF gene. It is extremely common. In a class of school children, at least one child will be a carrier of the CF gene; in a large business meeting, there is a chance that at least one person will be carrying the gene; in a rugby match it is likely that one player will be a carrier. But you do not know if you are a carrier of the CF gene unless you are tested for it, or if you produce a child who has CF. Many of us may be CF gene carriers without ever realising it. So, two CF gene carriers need to meet each other and then there is a one in four chance that their child will be born with CF.

The chances are the same (one in four) for each pregnancy and the condition affects boys and girls equally.

There are many different manifestations of CF from the very mild (many people walking around today with mild

CF may be totally unaware they have the condition) to moderate and severe effects of the condition. The severity of the illness may depend on the genetic mutation of the CF gene inherited from the parents.

The mechanics of CF are scientifically complex, so this book will not go into them in any great detail, but to put it simply, the salt and chloride channels in every cell in the body are affected to varying degrees, thus not allowing these substances to move freely. As a result, any mucus-producing area of the body will be affected by CF, mainly the lungs but also the gastrointestinal system and the reproductive system. In other words, three of the main bodily systems conducive to life - breathing, eating and reproducing - are affected. The heart and brain are usually completely normal.

The CF gene has over 1000 different mutations and more are being discovered all the time. Again, this is a complex area to explain, but it is an important one to understand especially with the new classes of medications that are emerging to treat the condition.

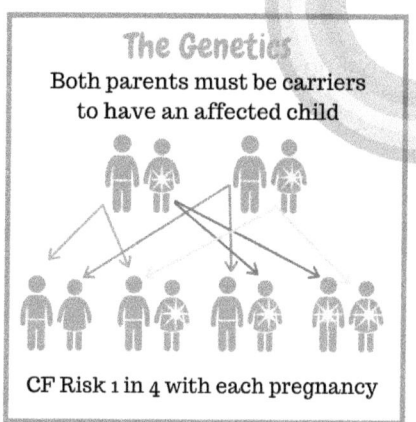

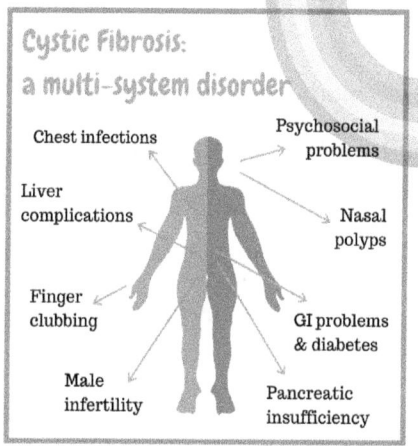

---

[1] With thanks to The Leanne Fund for allowing me to use their illustrations

The most common CF genetic mutation in the UK and Europe is one called Delta F508 (or F508del as it is now more commonly known). Approximately seventy percent of those with CF in the UK will have one inherited F508del mutation and around forty-eight percent will have F508del mutations for both of their inherited genes. There are many other commonly recognised mutations in CF and many will dictate the course of the disease, whether it be a mild or more severe manifestation of the condition.

New disease modifying precision drugs have been developed to treat CF over the last few years, therefore it is now vital for patients and health professionals to be aware and informed of their specific mutations, in order for the appropriate medication to be prescribed.

Symptoms of CF can be many and varied for each person. Every person with CF will be different and they can never be compared with each other. There are definite trends and patterns in the illness, and as health professionals, we can take a good guess as to the course of the condition for each of our patients, but this will depend on many factors including medication adherence, current age and stage of the patient, their genetic mutation and personality. Many of these things will vary depending on general life events and external stressors, meaning that it is usually impossible to accurately predict the future for each patient. This can be frustrating for patients and their families, especially in this day and age, when people like to know what the future holds and want to have things mapped out in front of them.

Impossible to do in CF!

CF mainly affects the lungs, although a baby with CF is usually born with perfectly normal organs. The chronic infections, inflammation and bacterial colonisation will cause lung damage over the years, which is why all CF teams try to prevent this from occurring from an early age. All bacteria thrive in the warm, moist and inviting atmosphere in the lungs - a perfect environment for them to flourish. Patients are experts in coughing up sputum and providing constant samples for the hospital labs to analyse and report on.

Throughout my nursing career, sputum has been one of the few things I have found difficult to come to terms with - thick, yellow or green slime, sometimes with all sorts of unidentifiable bits in it - even writing this makes me feel squeamish and nauseous. Yes, strange that I ended up in the field of CF, where expertise in sputum evaluation and identification is vital. Patients would often have their sputum pots on their bedside table next to their trays of lunch or supper and would take great pleasure in taking off the lids and showing the contents to me just after I had eaten my own lunch. But I always tried never to show my true reactions to this - to this day I hope none of the patients realised how horrified I was when the dreaded open pot was pointed in my direction.

However, for people with CF, sputum production and coughing are a daily part of their lives and they have often not known anything different. Bacteria, with scary sounding names such as *staphylococcus* and *pseudomonas* will often become colonised in the airways and lungs, resulting in thick, infected looking sputum and a chronic deep and painful sounding cough. Patients often tell stories of being on a train or in a classroom and receiving disapproving looks from other people as they try to contain their coughing, to make it sound less severe. I remember one patient saying that she dreaded going out for meals with her family because her father was prone to making jokes at the table. Every time she laughed, she became convulsed with coughing, which drew the unwanted attention and comments of the other diners in the restaurant. She said she ended up making excuses not to go out for meals with her family, pleading homework or not feeling well - for teenagers, experiences like this can be mortifying.

As well as having to endure the daily burden of coughing and excessive sputum production, acute chest infections are also part of life for someone with CF. Sometimes it is hard for a patient to distinguish between an acute exacerbation and the usual chronic symptoms, but clinically there maybe signs of increased coughing, sputum production and lethargy, as well as infection markers changing in the blood.

In recent times we are constantly being told that antibiotic usage has got out of hand and most day to day infections will resolve without the use of these medications. We are told this for good reasons; bacteria are clever in adapting, changing and becoming resistant to antibiotics. It is one of the biggest threats of our times and it would be disastrous to return to the days of pre-antibiotics when people frequently died of minor infections.

In CF, things are different. The bacteria inhabiting the lungs are strong and resilient and will often only respond to powerful antibiotics. In CF, we use eye-watering amounts of various antibiotics on a regular basis, with varying degrees of success. Bacterial pathogens are getting more resistant and it was not uncommon for the labs to send us reports stating that the particular strain of bacteria was resistant to every single antibiotic that it was tested against. It is known that combinations of more than one antibiotic tend to work better than single agents, so we often treat acute infections in our patients with a cocktail of strong intravenous antibiotics for a prolonged period of time. This is tough for patients who have frequent chest infections requiring such treatment; the disruption to their day-to-day lives is significant, especially if they also need to be in hospital for the duration of their regime.

Eventually, for most patients with CF, the lung damage and infections will claim their lives. Usually infections become more frequent and they become harder to treat. Hospital admissions become more regular and quality of life is diminished. Often, people with CF need to reduce their hours at work as their condition becomes overpowering and some will need to leave their independent lives and move back into the family home. It is a tough time for all concerned, but sadly, such can be the cruel nature of CF.

Lung transplantation is one treatment that offers real hope and promise, but it is not always an easy journey to embark upon. I will discuss lung transplantation later in this book - it is an emotive and complex topic and merits a chapter to itself.

More than half of babies with CF born today will live into their fifties according to a recent study, and with new drug developments it is envisaged that it may not be too long in the future before people with CF will have a normal life expectancy. When I first started working in the world of CF in the early 1990's, the median survival age was thirty-one. It is hard for anyone with a long-term condition to be confronted with a 'median' age of death. This particular number will become lodged in the mind and even when it was explained to our patients that half the CF population would live longer than this, it was hard for them to see past the age of thirty-one as the age of their death.

One patient, Simon, started to become depressed and disillusioned with life in his late twenty's. He had previously been a man who enjoyed life to the full; his CF was relatively mild; he had a full-time job and an active social life. He admitted to us at one of his clinic visits that he no longer felt any enjoyment from life and he did not know why. He had lost interest in his health and had stopped taking many of his medications. He had also started to have some suicidal thoughts which were frightening and unfamiliar to him. There did not seem to be any trigger or change in his circumstances that would account for this change of mood and so he reluctantly agreed to meet with our psychologist to explore his feelings further. After several consultations, our psychologist elicited from Simon that many years earlier, he had seen that he would only live to the age of thirty. When he had first read this information, it did not register significantly with him as he was in his early teens at that point and he was in the 'invincible stage' of adolescence. Now that he was in his twenty's, the age of 'thirty' loomed large and threateningly over his life. Subconsciously, he was burdened with the thought that he only had two or three years left to him. Normal day-to-day activities lost their interest for him and he had the overwhelming feeling that life was no longer worth living. Although it was a relief for him when the reason for these feelings was identified, it took a long time for Simon to come to terms with the situation. And, in fact, it was not until he was well into his thirty's that he was finally able to accept that he was still fit, healthy and probably had many years of fulfilling life ahead of him. He is now in his late forty's, is happily married and has a beautiful son. He remains healthy and well.

There are many manifestations of CF other than lung disease. These include digestive issues, diabetes, liver problems, bone thinning and reproductive problems, not to mention the psychological issues that will inevitably accompany such potentially devastating symptoms. These will all be discussed further in the book.

Although CF is such a complicated disorder, it must never be forgotten that, behind the clinical symptoms, there is a human being. Someone with thoughts, emotions, feelings and dreams just like anyone else. CF does not discriminate and can affect anybody in the whole cross-section of society. Those choosing to work in the field of caring for people with CF must be aware of this and they must be able to see the person in a holistic way; to understand that the care goes far beyond the chesty cough, the production of sputum or the cramping stomach.

Patients I have looked after over the years have agreed to be part of this book, so that I can show the human aspects behind the disease; to show that people with CF face their hopes, dreams, fears and adversity - just as we all do.

2

~ Millie's story ~

Millie is someone who has 'typical' CF. As typical as it is possible to be. She is now sixteen years old and lives at home with her mother and her older brother. She is currently at school and is studying for exams. She does not yet know what she wants to do after school.

She hates having CF. She has grown up with the condition and all her life she has needed to be seen every three months or so at the hospital. At each appointment, she is told that she must keep doing her treatments or she will become unwell. Every so often, a new treatment is added to her already burdensome regime and she is told she needs to take it twice a day, every day, for ever.

She hates doing these treatments - they take so long every day. She needs to get up extra early when she is at school so that she can take her nebulised (inhaled) antibiotics, her sputum-thinning nebuliser, her regular oral antibiotic, her pancreatic enzymes, her 'stomach coating' tablet - and then do her physiotherapy after all of this. All before school.

And again, when she gets home.

She hates being different from her friends. They get to lie in until the last minute before getting up for school. They often complain of a minor cough or cold. Although they may try to understand, no one knows exactly what it is like to have CF unless they live with it themselves.

Even the CF team at the hospital do not understand, especially when they seem so disappointed (and sometimes irritated) when they find out she has not taken all of her medication, all of the time.

The pancreatic enzymes are the worst. Millie needs to take these with every meal - sometimes up to ten capsules at a time. In front of all her friends. The more fat in the meal, the more enzymes she needs to take. This is because the naturally occurring enzymes, that would normally flow from her pancreas to her stomach to break down food, are unable to get through the thickened mucus to do their job. If she did not take supplemental enzymes, her food would pass straight through her without being properly digested, she would have diarrhoea, severe stomach cramps and she would lose weight very quickly.

Sometimes, Millie does not take these enzymes - in the school canteen in front of everyone? Maybe it would be better to face the consequences of the diarrhoea and cramps?

This is just one of the dilemmas that a teenager with CF may face. There are so many more. Adolescence is a tough time for young people, with or without CF, and this has been made worse in recent times by the pressures of social media. Peer groups are so important; adolescents are much more influenced by their friendship groups and peers than their parents, carers or other relatives.

This is very normal. One of my favourite lectures that I have presented over the years at various conferences and meetings has been entitled 'The Teenage Brain'. The changes that occur in the teenage brain during adolescence are fascinating and more is being discovered all the time, especially with the developing science of MRI scanning. I think all parents (whether they have a child with CF or not) need to be aware of these changes in the teenage brain, and to realise that the behaviour of these young people is not all hormone-driven. I became far more tolerant and understanding of my own teenage children's behaviour following my research for this talk. Although my eldest son tells me he doesn't remember this!

It is normal for teenagers to rebel during this stage; they feel 'invincible' (nothing bad can ever happen to me) and thus they are willing to engage in reckless and risky behaviour, such as smoking, drug taking and fast driving.

They will become sexually aware and they feel embarrassed (often mortified) of their parents' behaviour, especially in front of their friends. This is a phase of selfish attitudes, a 'me, me, me' culture, with little empathy or thought for others, especially the boring and unimportant parents.

This is a time of breaking away from the 'apron strings' - attempting to become independent and to start living in the real world. This can be hard for parents, and of course the 'empty nest syndrome' is well reported - this is far harder for parents than for the child.

As a parent, imagine all of this going on and, in addition, your child has CF. The endless hospital appointments, treatments to be undertaken and symptoms that need to be carefully monitored for signs of acute infections or any other CF related issue.

Adolescence is tough for parents of children who have CF. For years, parents have been the ones (usually) who have kept their child well. They have been the ones to ensure medications are taken, nebuliser machines have been washed, physiotherapy has been done and appointments have been attended.

Things change during adolescence. A child may change into a moody, angry, grumpy and belligerent young person. The parent may no longer have 'control' over them. Parents do not know if they have been taking their medications or not. Or if they have been doing their physiotherapy. Often, the parent will be aware that they need to start stepping back, they need to start giving their child a chance to take on their own treatment regimes and to start 'owning' their CF. But this must be so difficult for them.

Over the years, I have had many mothers and fathers at their wit's end in the clinic, desperately still wanting to help and be involved in their child's care but knowing that they need to retreat, for their child's own sake. Often during this time, a teenager's health may deteriorate. They will have been missing their medication, staying out late, drinking to excess and often much worse. They just want to be like their friends and they are bitterly resenting the fact they have CF. I have had many conversations with distraught parents, telling them that it is important, maybe imperative, that an adolescent goes through this stage; they need to be able to learn from their own mistakes and realise what may happen to their health if they do not take all their treatments. I am aware that this is easy for me to say - I have never been in the shoes of a parent watching their beloved child's health deteriorating and knowing they need to just stand back and watch.

Millie knows that her CF will not get better. She has lived with it all her life and does not know life without CF. She has access to as much information about CF as she needs on the internet, she may have friends with CF all over the world on social media, she may be on chat rooms with others also with CF and she will hear about what she may expect to face in the future. Events such as declining health, more frequent chest infections and the need for intravenous antibiotics. And of course, there is much on the internet about lung transplantation in CF; the good and the bad experiences. There are also plenty of stories and anecdotes about dying from CF - and most of these will involve people dying at a very young age.

Imagine how frightening this must be for someone who knows they may have this in front of them? Nobody wants to think about their own death, especially when they are just a teenager and should have their whole life ahead of them. It is no wonder that so many adolescents with CF start to bury their heads in the sand, begin to deny that they have a serious condition and pretend that nothing is wrong. Ignore their treatment regimes, enjoy life with their friends and begin to resent everything to do with their CF.

I have had many young patients sitting reluctantly in front of me, wishing they were anywhere but in the CF clinic. Eyes facing the desk and heads bowed. Not answering any of the questions we are asking and not divulging any information about themselves or their health. Occasionally we may get the odd grunt or nod of the head but often, we get nothing from them.

Do we blame them? Do we get annoyed and irritated? Do we feel we are wasting our time and get exasperated when we see the patient's health start to deteriorate in front of us? The answer is 'yes' to all of these questions! But ... we need to remember that we were all teenagers once. And most of us did not have the burden of living with CF as well. How many of us have not finished a course of antibiotics? And this would probably only have been a short five to seven day course of just one or two tablets. How many of us (including me) do not take our asthma medication everyday? And we are asking (telling) our patients to do some much more than this ... every day of their lives. I do not believe that anyone can do one hundred percent of their treatment one hundred percent of the time. And I strongly feel that if a health professional working with people with CF does not empathise with this, then they should probably be working within some other discipline.

~ ... ~

Millie is sixteen and this is the age when, in most UK CF centres, patients will 'transition' from the children's clinic to the adult clinic.

I believe that the age of sixteen is one of the worst times to have to move from the familiar, child-friendly paediatric service to the larger, more scary and unfamiliar adult service. A totally different clinic, often a different hospital with a whole different CF team. So much is going on in the life of a sixteen-year-old teenager, including exams, adolescence, peer pressure, difficult parental relationships and just discovering who you really are. And now, on top of this, we are asking these teenagers to leave behind the CF team that they may have known all their lives, where everything is 'safe and trusted'. And it is hard for parents and carers too. It is no wonder that when new patients and families come to the adult clinic for the first time, the staff are often viewed with suspicion and resentment.

Transition in CF has been the subject of much debate and research over the years and there have never been any definitive answers regarding the best way to manage it. Each CF centre in the UK may have their own ways of doing this and will differ from each other. No method is perfect, but each centre will do the best that they can and will try to learn from each other as well as reviewing and implementing any up-to-date and convincing research. The overall aim is to make the transition pathway as smooth and easy as possible for the young patients with CF and their families.

When I started working in CF in 1993, there was an elderly respiratory paediatrician who was based in the children's hospital adjacent to the adult CF centre. His philosophy was to chat to patients and their families just about one or two months prior to transition. He would tell them it was time to move up to the adult hospital and he would not be seeing them again. He would write a comprehensive transfer letter to the adult team and the subsequent appointment for the patient would be in the adult centre, with no other preparation or information. Patients were usually around fourteen years of age and it probably was a nerve-wracking time for them. However, in my experience, the transition of these patients happened without too much trauma. Parents and carers were usually more anxious about it than the patient themselves. But it was often the thought of transition that was worse than the actual event itself.

There is something to be said for a swift, no nonsense transition in that it just happens. There is no time for too much anxiety or deliberation - for one appointment you are at the children's clinic, for the next you are at the adult centre.

However, the general trend now is that patients with CF will transition around the age of sixteen, with about two years preparation for this. At our centre, transition clinics were held every six months with both the paediatric and adult teams in attendance. Towards the end of the transition period, more of the clinics were held at the adult centre to familiarise the patient and family to the new environment.

Both methods have their advantages, but from experience, I would say that transition is a tricky time for families however it is done. But usually the patient settles in quickly to the new centre and often they would admit that it was the whole idea and thought of the transition that was much worse than the actual move itself.

~ ... ~

Millie's mother, Sue, was finding this teenage period of Millie's life really difficult. Millie had become more distant from her and was spending long periods of time in her room with the door shut. She was constantly attached to her phone and seemed to have more of a social life 'speaking' to people via social media than actually physically going out with friends. The old days of chatting to each other after school and going shopping together had gone and Sue had no idea how much of her CF treatment Millie was doing. Millie's cough had got worse and Sue spent many long hours in the middle of the night listening to the constant coughing and retching, which sometimes led to physical vomiting. Both were tired and irritable in the morning which led to even more fractious relations. Trying to discuss matters relating to CF was becoming impossible and Sue felt that at times Millie was a complete stranger.

One of Sue's main concerns is that she would be 'excluded' from Millie's care once she was attending the adult centre. This was a common fear, and one that was not unique to our centre. As a team, we always worked hard to dispel these fears and, providing the patient agreed, we tried to ensure that parents and carers were included in all aspects of care initially following transition.

The first few appointments following Millie's transition were interesting but not unusual. Sue was nervous and emotional at times, and was keen to do most of the talking; Millie was quiet, head bowed low and she looked, understandably, that she would rather be anywhere other than the clinic. Over the next few months, Millie gradually began to get used to the new centre, she began to smile at members of the team when we greeted her, and occasionally she even volunteered information on her own! Sue began to take a back seat in the consultation and allowed Millie time to answer questions herself. After a while, Millie asked (or maybe told) Sue to wait in the waiting room so that Millie could be seen on her own. This is a significant step forward and one that often shows that a patient is beginning to mature and move on from the adolescent phase. For some patients, this takes only weeks and for others it can take years. We still had some forty-year-old patients who liked their mothers to come into the clinic room with them.

For me, one of the most satisfying parts of the job was to see a patient move, over the years, from a silent and often moody adolescent to a fully-fledged mature adult, taking full responsibility for their own CF and treatment.

3
~ My story ~

This book is not about me. However, it may be interesting for you to know a little about my nursing career and how I ended up in the field of CF.

I started my nursing training in January 1980. I had been accepted for the course at The London Hospital, in Whitechapel (known as The Royal London Hospital today). I had been living with my parents and four brothers in Kent, where I had what could be described as a relatively middle-class and privileged life.

My father was a Civil Engineer specialising in water treatment works and this job took him all over the world to countries such as Malaysia and Sri Lanka. Indeed, I spent around six years of my early childhood in Malaysia and one of my brothers was born out there.

My mother was a doctor and for the latter years of her career had worked as a GP in a fairly deprived area of Kent. Our house was a busy, noisy place filled with music and social activities. All of my brothers were talented at maths and music but unfortunately, I had not inherited this particular gene. I tried hard at the piano and clarinet, but was delighted when I was allowed to give up my lessons. My maths achievements were non-existent and I was very relieved when I got a C in my O level, which meant I had reached the grades I needed to get into nurse training. I was happy to throw away my maths texts books and calculator for good.

So, at the age of eighteen, I left this comfortable lifestyle and moved to the gritty East End of London.

~ ... ~

It took me a while to settle into this new environment; I was living in an austere and sterile nurses' home, with a scary and intimidating bird-like lady called Lottie who sat at the front desk behind a big glass window. She had an eagle-eye for the comings and goings of all the junior student nurses and woe betide anyone even considering bringing a friend from the opposite sex into the home. There were regular middle-of-the-night fire alarms and often sheepish, red-faced males accompanied us out onto the cold and wet streets outside the home at four in the morning.

Nursing was predominantly a female profession even in the 1980's and male nurses were few and far between. I can only remember coming across one or two male student nurses during my training; it is of course very different today. The nurses home felt like a combination of a strict all-girls boarding school and a convent, neither of which I had prior experience of.

We all had single bedrooms but each floor had to share a tiny, outdated kitchen and an antiquated bathroom - the size of the bath was enormous, it would have been luxurious if there had ever been enough hot water to fill it.

My nurse training was generally enjoyable and uneventful. I genuinely think that the NHS was a happier environment to work in during those days. Patients were usually less unwell, there was less technology and machinery geared to keeping people alive, the nurses were less stressed and the wards were usually well-staffed and more relaxed than they are today. Patients still got excellent care, but there was a different atmosphere in the hospital. Staff helped each other out. On one occasion, I remember having a very early flight to Greece whilst I was on night duty and two of the day staff came on duty at 4am to allow me to leave to catch the plane. Not sure if this would happen nowadays?

We played innocuous tricks on each other, often with the patient's involvement and to their delight. We once attached a patient to a fake intravenous drip and put a small carrot, shaped into a goldfish, in the infusion bag.

It was funny to see the carrot 'swimming' about and even funnier to see how long it would take for the consultant to notice it. The patients loved it, and I really believe these things made their hospital stays more bearable.

As a brand-new student nurse on my very first placement on a male surgical ward, I was given a "paediatric" admission sheet to go through, with a patient who was in for a routine minor operation. When I got to the question, which was obviously intended for a young child: *'do you have a special comforter you use at night?'* I paused and thought before I continued. I still cannot believe I actually asked the question - it proves that at that time I just blindly did as I was told. I said to the poor gentleman: *'This might sound a bit odd but it is one of the questions that I need to ask... Do you have a special comforter you use at night?'*. The man did not hesitate for one second as he replied in his broad cockney accent: *'only the wife!'* and I duly wrote down his answer in the space provided.

~ ... ~

After my training, I initially worked in the special care baby unit (too stressful for me), before moving to the Accident and Emergency (A&E) Department. I loved this department and learnt so much. Every day was different and I saw life at its best and worst. This was probably the first time that I had worked within a team where doctors, nurses and other health professionals were treated equally and with respect for one another. Junior doctors looked to the more experienced nurses for help and advice when they first started in the department, and this was refreshing and also ahead of its time, even for the mid 1980's. There was a great team atmosphere in this unit, a comradeship that was not dented by even the most gruelling and violent of injuries we treated. It was a good example of a true multidisciplinary team and one that I often referred back to during my years of working in CF.

We definitely saw all sorts in this department; a busy A&E in a major teaching hospital in the depths of East London - this was before the days of the affluent middle classes who moved to the area over the following decades. You never knew who or what would come through the doors next and this kept the adrenaline levels high, making good team work imperative. I learnt a huge amount about life and death, and saw things maybe a twenty-one year-old should not see, but I will never forget my time there and enjoyed every minute.

I almost did not get this staff nurse job in A&E. I had worked there as a student nurse, so I knew the senior staff well. I had never been to an interview before and was very naive. When I was given the post, the senior sister said to me: '*You were lucky to get this job... you looked like you were dressed for Brighton Beach! We thought you were going to get changed into your bikini at any minute!*'. I had worn a bright stripy skirt and canvas espadrilles (very popular at the time) to the interview. I have thought long and hard about what to wear for interviews I have attended since.

~ ... ~

After eighteen months in A&E, I moved to one of the most unusual wards I have worked on. I still think of this ward often and, right up until the day I retired, I would try to ensure that I nursed to the standards that were the normal day-to-day expectations of this ward. Currie ward was a gastroenterology ward, specialising in liver issues. There were many patients who had regular and prolonged admissions to the ward and we got to know them very well. It was my first taste of chronic conditions in patients and I found it good to see familiar faces and to get to know more about the real people behind the clinical problems. At this stage, little did I know that I would go on to spend the largest part of my career looking after people with CF, whom I would also get to know incredibly well.

Currie ward was run by a Charge Nurse named Clive, who, though was eccentric and quirky, was inspirational. He treated everyone in exactly the same way, from the domestic staff to the consultants. Each week, one member of the ward team had to bring in a cake (preferably baked themselves) and on a Tuesday afternoon everyone met in the teaching room and enjoyed that week's creation. All but essential work stopped for that time and the whole team gathered to chat and have a brief respite from the ward. It was always amusing to see what type of cake the slightly old-fashioned male consultants brought in when it was their turn (although often they had persuaded their long-suffering wives to bake).

Clive was an unusual manager who allowed all his nursing staff to have five 'stress' days off in the year. These were days when the nurses could take an unofficial day off if we were feeling as if things had become too much and we needed a break from the ward for a day. Senior managers did not know about these days - they were managed between us by covering for each other. However, because the atmosphere on the ward was so relaxed, we rarely needed to take these 'days' - it was just reassuring to know they were there if we required them. I did not take a single 'stress day' in the eighteen months I was on this ward (just took the early morning flight to Greece, thanks to the help from my colleagues).

It was on Currie ward that I worked with another of the best colleagues I have ever been fortunate enough to meet. Harriet was a wonderful nurse. Nothing was too much effort as far as patients were concerned: if Phyllis wanted a cup of tea, Harriet would leave the paperwork she was engrossed in to fetch one; if Eddie needed a bottle, one was produced within seconds; if Bill was feeling low, Harriet would spend time sitting with him holding his hand and talking with him. These are all part of general every day nursing duties, but Harriet had the gift of making everyone feel special, as if they were the only patients on the ward and she was solely there for them.

One patient, Elsie, was a lovely old lady who had been on Currie ward for many months. She was one of those characters only found in the East End of London - a born and bred cockney lady with a wicked sense of humour. We all had a soft spot for Elsie, but Harriet especially loved her. Every morning, Harriet brought in *Mr Kipling's Fondant Fancies* for Elsie, who adored them, and she would eat them three at a time (these still make me think of Elsie whenever I see them). Elsie had beautiful long grey hair and it was one of her pleasures to have it washed and styled by one of the nurses on a daily basis (these were the days of the NHS when we did seem to have more time). Harriet loved to do this for Elsie and it was a time of the day when they laughed and chatted together, like old friends.

The time came when Elsie had to be transferred to the local care home in Hackney. It was a sad day for all of us when Elsie was wheeled away in her chair to get into the ambulance that was to take her to her new home. Harriet accompanied her and we all watched them head off into the distance.

A few weeks later, Harriet and I went to visit Elsie in the care home. She looked small and insignificant sitting in the huge armchair lined up with a number of the other residents, all staring at the wall opposite. She had lost the eager, mischievous eyes that had always been sparkling with humour and she did not even react to the box of *Fondant Fancies* that Harriet had brought her. The saddest thing of all was that her luscious long hair, always so beautifully styled, had been crudely and roughly chopped. When we asked the staff why this had been done, they said it was because it made things easier for them. I have never seen Harriet so angry - her normally calm and serene composure disappeared and she showed a flash of the temper I never realised she had. We returned to the ward feeling deflated and flat. It took Harriet a long time to get over what had happened to Elsie in the home. She continued to visit Elsie on a regular basis until she died a few months later.

These were happy times for me and I thrived on Currie ward. In 1986, some senior power from above decided that one ward in the hospital needed to close, in order to make cuts. What a surprise - Currie ward was selected. I think the senior management felt threatened by Clive and his maverick methods and the easiest way to solve this was to close the ward. This was devastating for all of us - staff and patients. Many petitions were signed and there was much publicity in the local papers, but to no avail. Currie ward was duly closed, Clive moved to a new job in the north of England, we were all redeployed. I never saw Clive again and he did not keep in touch with anybody from the ward as far as I knew. But his work ethos and team management skills have stayed with me always and I will be forever grateful to him.

~ ... ~

I became disillusioned with the NHS following the closure of Currie ward and left the hospital soon after. I spent some time setting up a knitting business - I had been left some money by my grandmother and I bought a knitting machine with this small legacy. All day long, I would work at my machine, creating guernsey sweaters which I sold at a stall in Camden Market at the weekends. This was a lonely job during the week and the machine was so noisy that it was impossible to even listen to the radio. Orders came in thick and fast and it was becoming very difficult to keep up with demand, so the whole enterprise became rather stressful.

So, I moved on to my next venture, which was to work as a nurse/ stewardess/ secretary on a multi-million-pound motor yacht based in the Mediterranean. My yachting tales are many and varied and will not be recounted in this book - maybe another time. It was an extraordinary period of my life and a very welcome distraction from the bureaucracy and dictates of the NHS.

~ ... ~

On returning to the UK, I worked for a short time at a private hospital before moving to the Homerton Hospital. This was a newly built general hospital in Hackney, part of St Bartholomew's. My position here was that of Relief Ward Sister, covering the surgical, orthopaedic and A&E departments. Of these three departments, I loved working in the surgical ward. I felt at home on Lamb ward, had a great team of nurses and got on well with the consultants and patients.

The surgical ward was very different from Currie ward. On Currie, the patients returned again and again, often with a flare up of their liver issues due to excess alcohol drinking. We even had one refined and well-to-do lady who left Currie ward several times on a Sunday to attend various different churches in the area to take the communion wine. She understood that she was not allowed to drink alcohol, but thought that communion wine was exempt. Conversely, the patients on Lamb ward were admitted and discharged relatively quickly, never to be seen by us again. Usually, they had their surgery and were 'fixed'. Because of this, they were usually very grateful and the nurse's station was always laden with boxes of chocolates and multiple thank you cards. It was a different way of nursing; one that was immensely satisfying and much easier on my back. The back pain that afflicts so many nurses, completely disappeared for me on Lamb ward.

I enjoyed being in a more senior position, giving me the opportunity to have a bit more control over the way the ward was run. I had definitely gained inspiration from Clive and Currie ward and I was determined to create the same cohesive team atmosphere as I had previously experienced. In the NHS in those days, it was probably easier to do this than it is now. Then, it was possible to be more relaxed, have team gatherings in the staff room each morning, with coffee and toast for all, and also to provide a flexible and empathetic way of working. Nowadays, the various constraints placed upon staff working on busy acute wards are very stringent, and this of course includes the usual issue of staff shortages. Low morale is, without any doubt, a serious problem in the NHS today; this makes it very difficult to facilitate the more relaxed, yet still excellent, nursing care we were able to give to our patients in the 1980s.

~ ... ~

Following a brief spell as an Infection Control Nurse Specialist at the Homerton Hospital, covering maternity leave, I moved onto work for The Imperial Cancer Research Fund (now known as Cancer Research UK). I was appointed as the lead Research Nurse on a national study looking into Malignant Melanoma. This was a hundred miles away from running a busy acute surgical ward, but I relished the change and the different challenges this position brought. Part of my role involved travelling the length and breadth of the UK visiting families who had been afflicted by melanoma, asking them a series of questions and then counting every mole on their bodies. I constantly thought, slept and dreamt about moles. I became obsessed with them and would scour the arms of everyone I met, either through work or socially, to see whether they might have any 'dysplastic naevi' (abnormal looking moles) on their skin. Although this might sound somewhat tedious, it was extraordinary how fascinated others were with this fetish and how they were very keen to get their own moles scrutinised and to be subsequently reassured that they did not have any that looked suspicious. Getting sunburnt was a complete no-no and totally against the message we were giving to our families; this was difficult for me as a person who loves hot and sunny holidays.

~ ... ~

It was during this time that I met Tim. My future husband, rock, best friend and father to my children. Over the years

I had fallen for many different men, many of them doctors I am somewhat embarrassed to say. I had had my heart broken (or sometimes just scratched) many times and had generally enjoyed my years of being intermittently 'single'. I met Tim at a mutual friend's party one evening in August 1989. He was the archetypal tall, dark and handsome man, but was also interesting to talk to. He told me he was a geologist, which sounded very romantic to me - until a friend told me a few weeks later that *'it's not romantic at all - a rock is just a rock'*.

Little did I know at this time, that my encounter with Tim would take me to live in the opposite end of the country and away from my beloved East End of London where I had spent so many happy years, both in nursing and socially.

After a year's long-distance relationship, with Tim in the north-east of Scotland and me in London, I gave up my job as a research nurse, sold my flat, followed him to Scotland and took the plunge into the unknown.

~ ... ~

After initially training as a district nurse, when I first moved to Scotland, I worked in a variety of nursing jobs, including a role as a research nurse in the respiratory department of a large teaching hospital working on an asthma study. It was whilst I was working in this job that I heard of the advertisement for a Cystic Fibrosis Specialist Nurse for a newly formed adult CF Unit in the hospital. I had no experience at all of nursing anyone with CF, although I did remember a nursing friend's brother had died of it in London a few years before. I did not apply for the job initially, but when it was re-advertised, I thought I would go for it. I was fortunate enough to be given the job and so I stepped forward into the world of CF.

4
~ The new Adult CF Centre ~

Everybody will come across people during their lifetimes who inspire and influence them in their day-to-day work. During my nursing career, I met a handful of people who did this. Of course, I worked with so many people who were wonderful nurses and doctors, as well as other members of the teams I was involved with, but a few stood out to me as role models.

Professor James Friend was one of these people. He had worked in the respiratory department for many years and was truly loved and respected by all who worked with him and especially by his patients. Once he retired, he even had a room at the hospital named after him (much to his embarrassment) - it is called the James Friend Room and hosts meetings, teaching sessions, goodbye parties and the annual Christmas quiz.

Professor Friend was kind and humble. He was a true gentleman and a gentle man. We all said that his surname was perfect for him - he really was a 'friend' to all. He became involved in every aspect of his patient's lives and saw each patient as a whole person, with a life beyond the complaint that had brought them to the hospital that day. He practiced holistic medicine in the truest sense of the word. I remember being alongside him one day as he was telling a patient that there was nothing more we could do for them and they were reaching the end of their lives. The way he conveyed these life-changing words to the patient was compassionate and heartfelt. When the patient became tearful, Professor Friend became emotional too; he was so engrossed in the moment - at that time, no one else mattered except for the patient lying in the bed whose life had just been changed for ever. An immensely special quality in a doctor, to be able to treat every single patient as a unique and individual human being.

Professor Friend was passionate about CF and in the late 1980's, he ran a monthly CF clinic where he saw a handful of young patients and reviewed their care. There was not a 'CF team' at this time, and he managed the care of these patients largely on his own. In those days, the treatment of CF was simpler: antibiotics, enzyme supplements and physiotherapy were the main recommendations - there were no nebulised medications, mucolytics (sputum thinning drugs) or portable oxygen therapy. The median age of survival for someone with CF in the 1980's was less than twenty years old.

There were only a few adult CF centres in the UK in those days, mainly because patients did not survive into adulthood. Most patients died whilst they were still being seen at the paediatric hospital. The first adult CF centre in Europe was established at The Brompton Hospital in London in 1965, but it was many years until all of the major hospitals in the UK could boast their own adult units. However, it was gradually recognised that this was a necessary part of treatment for CF, as patients with CF were living longer and were beginning to reach adulthood.

Adult centres in both Edinburgh and Glasgow were set up in the early 1990's, funded by ring-fenced monies from the Scottish Government under the auspices of the National Services Division (part of the Scottish Executive). All patients with CF in Scotland were expected to be reviewed at these centres at least annually, being seen at their local district hospitals in between times.

Scotland is sparsely populated outside the central belt; it is a large country and travelling from the north-east to the two main centres at that time was stressful and time consuming for patients and their families. Professor Friend felt strongly that the north-east corner of Scotland also warranted its own adult CF centre and fought hard to achieve this. He tells the story that the senior management staff at the hospital at the time were against this development, for reasons best known to themselves, but he persevered and in 1993, he won his battle. The National Services Division awarded the hospital a significant amount of money to set up its own adult CF centre.

I joined the service in 1993, and at that time there were twenty-four patients attending the clinic. The multidisciplinary team was small at this point, but Professor Friend was joined by another consultant, Dr Joe Legge - another of my inspirational colleagues, who also had a passion for CF. Professor Friend and Dr Legge had known each other for a long time, had worked together for years and had great mutual respect and admiration for each other. Professor Friend was kind, humble and unassuming whereas Dr Legge was dynamic, efficient and wise. They made a wonderful team - their skills complemented each other perfectly and above all, they both had a great sense of humour. I was so fortunate to have worked with them both, and I am privileged to still have their friendship today, long after they have both retired.

These were exciting times in the world of CF. In 1989, the CF gene defect had been discovered by a team of researchers, led by Dr Lap-Chee Tsui, in Canada. Today, the genes for many conditions have been identified, but CF was the first disease-causing gene to be found, so its discovery was of great significance. Research into gene therapy treatment for CF has been going on for many years, with ups and downs in its findings and journey. We were told from an early stage that a breakthrough was imminent and treatment would be available in around "ten years" from now. Patients and families naturally pinned great hope on this treatment and expectations were high.

~ ... ~

I remember when I had not been in the job very long, a young boy called Carl and his mother were in the clinic. Carl was about sixteen years old and his mother was slightly overbearing and extremely protective towards him. We were discussing gene therapy and they were very excited about what they thought was a fast-approaching viable treatment. Naively, I just repeated to them what I had heard recently at a conference I had been to - that treatment with gene therapy was around 'ten years' away from being in daily use for people with CF.

I was unprepared for the reaction I got. They were devastated to hear this. The relationship between us changed immediately and Carl's mother became distant and openly hostile towards me. Shortly after they left the clinic, Carl's mother phoned and spared no words in telling me that I had taken away all hope from Carl for gene therapy treatment and how dare I do this. Who did I think I was, as a junior CF nurse recently in post, to act and talk as if I was the 'expert' in CF care and gene therapy research? She did not think that Carl had ten years to live and the family had kept his hopes alive with the prospect of a treatment for CF that could change the condition and keep it at bay.

She was furious with me and I was mortified. She may have overreacted to this situation, but I never forgot it and it taught me a significant lesson. She was purely being a mother who loved her son so much and would protect him at any cost. 'Hope' is such an important aspect of living with a chronic condition and who was I to take this away from someone? There is a fine balance between living with the reality of the situation while also maintaining hope, and it is a balance that we do not get right all of the time. But this experience taught me to always think carefully before pronouncing on any situation and to weigh up the balance between dashing hope and also being realistic. Carl's mother was right - Carl did not have ten years left to him; he died at the age of twenty-one. And to this day, over twenty years later, gene therapy is unfortunately still not yet a viable treatment option for CF, although research continues.

~ ... ~

I loved the early days in my role as a CF nurse specialist. The Respiratory Unit was based at that time in a small cottage hospital on the edge of the city and there was a family-like atmosphere. Everyone knew each other and it was a friendly and informal place to work. I had time to develop the role and I really enjoyed getting to know the patients and their families. The year before I took up the post was a tough year for Professor Friend, as five of his patients with CF had died, including siblings from the same family. This must have been difficult for everyone;

especially as palliative care services had also not been fully developed at this point. As a result, the patients I looked after when I started were relatively well for the first few years and my workload was comparatively light.

~ ... ~

The first CF death that I experienced was Pamela who was thirty-eight years old. In those days, this was considered 'elderly' for someone with CF and she had lived long enough to see her son become a teenager, which was also unusual. Looking back on her death, I feel that there were many things which could have been done better. Pamela's health had been slowly declining for many months and her quality of life at the end was severely diminished. I had been in the post for about three years at this point and had not yet seen a death from CF. I did not know what to expect or how to support Pamela and her family. Home oxygen therapy was not available at this time and it was hard to see her struggling to breathe. Her end of life wishes were not discussed or even referred to, and I am not sure that anyone ever had an open and honest talk with her about her prognosis. Her son's needs were not taken into account and he was rarely seen with her, as he was always 'busy' elsewhere. I still wonder today how he is and whether he managed to get through that incredibly difficult time without too many psychological scars. In addition to her son, Pamela's mother lived with her too and she was totally bewildered by the whole process of watching her daughter die.

When I think of the palliative care and end of life services that are available today and how the field has developed, I wish that we had been able to offer some of these to Pamela. I hope that she died with dignity and peace, but I know that things could have been done better to prepare her and her family for her death, and that thought can still haunt me today.

5
~ Working in a multidisciplinary team ~

It is known that a multidisciplinary team (MDT) approach is the best way to give optimum care to patients with long-term, chronic conditions. Patients are able to access a range of expertise, such as medical staff, specialist nurses, physiotherapists, dieticians, social workers and psychologists. Today, many patients with conditions such as diabetes and heart conditions are being cared for by MDTs and this is a positive development in health care. Effective MDT working enables the patient to be involved in their own care and to take some control over their treatment and outcomes. From the team point of view, MDT working allows different areas of expertise to work together and to look at each patient in a holistic way.

With mutual respect and good communication, working in a dynamic MDT can be one of the most satisfying ways to provide the best medical care for our patients.

The field of CF is a good example of the success of MDTs. It is known that the survival rate of patients with CF has increased significantly over the years, and this is largely due to the development of specialist centres and provision of MDT care. CF was one of the first long-term conditions to utilise MDT working and it is now a well-established and expected part of CF care.

In 1993, when I first began working in the field of CF, our MDT was in the initial stages of development, led by Professor James Friend and Dr Joe Legge. I was the first specialist nurse in the respiratory department - today this department is home to multiple specialist nurses: in asthma, bronchoscopy, lung cancer, sleep conditions and chronic obstructive pulmonary disorder, to name just a few. The world of the specialist nurse is now an established discipline and this role is an invaluable addition to any MDT.

Our initial team comprised two respiratory consultants, a nurse specialist, a physiotherapist and a dietician. We cared for twenty-four patients at that time and we worked together to give the best possible care to this small but complex group. We were able to get to know the patients and their families incredibly well and it was a privilege to be involved in their lives.

I was given additional support from other CF nurses within Scotland and we met on a regular basis in various parts of the country every three months or so. I remember, with gratitude, the help they gave me when I first started. We were all relatively new in post and were all experiencing similar issues – it was a little like the 'blind leading the blind', but we were able to share protocols, discuss problems and generally be there for each other. Like myself, many of those initial Scottish CF nurses also remained in post for more than two decades and they became close friends. It is strange now that we are all on the brink of retirement ourselves - these years of long-term expertise will be a significant loss for the world of CF, but we know that those following in our footsteps will step into our shoes without too much difficulty and will continue our dedication to this special group of patients.

Mutual respect and good communication are crucial to a good MDT working environment. In an ideal world, everyone would work closely together, listen to each other, bounce ideas off each other and generally co-exist in a wispy cloud of dynamism and happiness. In reality, this rarely happens, although glimpses of this 'utopia' do occur from time to time. You can imagine trying to work under the strains of the NHS umbrella, with staff shortages, resource limitations, day-to-day stresses, demanding patients, exacting doctors and multiple time constraints - all part of daily life. On top of this, there could be difficult personality clashes, large egos, personal stress at home and the feeling that others are not pulling their weight within the team. These are normal and real situations, but the key is how they are dealt with. It is not always easy, but it is essential to try to work through these difficulties before they become irresolvable. Usually such issues can be sorted, either formally or (more commonly) informally. In our team, we found that regular team 'nights out' were helpful - an occasional evening away from the hospital, a good meal and some alcohol seemed to allow everyone to let their hair down and just enjoy each other's company. The general chat and camaraderie following these events lasted several days afterwards at work and patients also enjoyed hearing about them. Sometimes, however, the unsettled seams of discomfort ran deeper within the team, demanding a more formal resolution.

~ ... ~

I had a difficult issue with a colleague many years ago, when I was pregnant with my third child. Even now, I find it hard to talk and write about it. In my mind, the problem seemed to blow up from nowhere, but for her, things had been brewing for a long time. I was totally unaware that she had issues with me and my management style; maybe this reflects my naivety at that time, but I certainly learnt from this experience and after this was always very sensitive regarding the complexities of team working. Unfortunately, this particular colleague raised her concerns about me just a week before I was going off for my maternity leave. She put in a formal complaint about me and it ended up being dealt with by senior management. It was a difficult time, as nothing could be effectively resolved while I was not at work. But I refused to return to work from my maternity leave without addressing the situation. This resulted in multiple meetings with management and my union representative during my maternity leave - this whole experience without doubt had a massive impact on the enjoyment of my new baby and I am sure my fluctuating hormones did not help my stress levels in any way! I will not go into any of the details of my colleague's complaints about me, but suffice it to say that a 'disciplinary hearing' was held shortly before I was due to return to work. Every single one of her claims against me was unsubstantiated, she was removed from the team and redeployed to another area in the hospital.

I never saw her again.

Although I was totally exonerated, it was a difficult time and one that will stay with me for ever. On returning to work following my maternity leave, I perceived that my situation had been the main topic of conversation for the rest of the team for the previous eight months (how paranoid of me!) - of course, in reality, the team had just been working away as normal and battling with the usual everyday stresses and strains of the job. Most of the team had been supportive to me over this period and I will be eternally grateful to them for this. However, I felt that I still needed to justify myself and my position within the team, although I think this was mainly to satisfy my own insecurities rather than for any other reason. I was hypersensitive about not upsetting anyone and I became fairly introverted for a long time for fear of appearing too controversial or controlling. It took some time for me to feel that the rest of the team accepted me as a valuable and respected member once again.

~ ... ~

Over the years I have been involved in several disciplinary cases, where others have been the main focus of attention. Some of these were justified, others were not, but following my own experience, I was always aware of the stress and anxiety such disputes can cause for all involved. Whilst I understand that sufficient time must be given over to ensuring all aspects of any disciplinary case are fair and just, I think that such situations need to be concluded in a more timely manner - some cases can go on for months and months, which surely only adds to the distress for everyone.

Generally, my experience of working within an MDT has been a positive one. It is a privilege to work with experts in other disciplines and there is no doubt that patients benefit from this collaborative working method. Although there will inevitably be team members coming and going, generally our CF team remained fairly stable. I have worked with some of my colleagues within the team for over ten years, which means we get to know each other extremely well. It is imperative that everyone within the team has an equal voice and that all opinions are treated with respect and consideration. Large egos need to be kept under control and impending issues need to be addressed quickly and efficiently.

It must be recognised that there will always be ups and downs within each team and it most definitely is not all plain sailing, but this is no different from every aspect of living in the real world. Working so closely within a relatively small MDT, where we are so intricately involved with the patient group, is similar to living within a family - there will be arguments, differences of opinions and occasional backstabbing, but we all manage to respect and tolerate each other in the end.

6
~ Boundaries ~

All practising health professionals will have clear rules and regulations set out by their professional bodies, outlining duties and responsibilities to patients, carers and colleagues. As nurses, we are bound by the Nursing and Midwifery Council Code of Professional Conduct - a twenty-four-page document, which is regularly reviewed and updated as necessary.

Section 20 of the Code of Professional Conduct is entitled "Uphold the reputation of your profession at all times" and contains the following clause:

'stay objective and have clear professional boundaries at all times with people in your care (including those who

have been in your care in the past), their families and carers'.

This is a clear statement, advising nurses to remain professional and impartial at all times and to be aware of where relationship boundaries with patients begin and end. This is difficult in all areas of health care; there will always be patients that 'could have been good friends' in other spheres of life. And what about more distant relatives of patients, are the same boundary rules applied here? Where do these boundaries lie? Who is to judge where boundaries lie and when they have been crossed? Sometimes there are clear breaches of this clause - a good friend of mine in London married one of her patients and I also know of a CF nurse who married one of her patients (she left her post immediately) - but where does human involvement and care become a 'crossing of the boundary'?

In CF this is particularly difficult and, without any doubt, boundaries become blurred on a regular basis. The CF team and CF patients get to know each other extraordinarily well - this is inevitable as CF is a chronic condition and we are alongside the patients and families through good times and bad. The average CF patient is seen approximately every three months at the clinic, although many of them are seen much more regularly. The various team members visit patients and families at home so we get to see them in their own surroundings and at their most relaxed state. We are guests in their homes, they will offer us tea and coffee (one particular patient always made us soup whenever we visited), we sit on their sofas and stroke their pets. This relationship will obviously be different to nursing a patient on an acute medical ward in the hospital and talking to relatives in a sterile, clinical room or by the bedside.

By the time I retired, I had known many of the CF patients and families for well over twenty years. How can the stereotypical nurse/patient relationship be maintained after all this time? I defy anyone with a heart not to have become involved with these patients and their families after so many years.

Many of the patients also knew all about me - my family, my holidays, which particular child was causing me angst at any time and many were so supportive at times such as when my father died six hundred miles away. Is this crossing a boundary? I believe that the patients wanted to know about me and my life, they enjoyed hearing about various stories that involved my children - it made more of an equal relationship in a long-term situation.

I hope that I was always professionally aware of such boundaries and would realise if there had been any risk of an obvious line being crossed. Although I occasionally met patients or a carer outside of the work environment, such as at a café, this was always as part of my CF role and not as a friend. A more relaxed, informal setting, on mutual territory, was sometimes the most conducive place for a particular situation.

Visiting patients at home was a significant part of my role and one that was very important. Nothing can substitute for seeing a patient in their home environment; meeting the dog they loved so much and experiencing some of the issues they were concerned about, such as lack of heating or mould growing around the bath. Sometimes, it was helpful and insightful to see how cramped the living conditions were and that there was just no space to store all the 'CF treatment' equipment: nebuliser machines, vials and vials of medication for intravenous antibiotic use, boxes of syringes and needles, plastic bins to throw used needles into, piles of tablets and general CF paraphernalia. Often three to four cupboards were required specifically to store all of this; sometimes a whole room was given over to it.

As well as noting the environment and general atmosphere in the patient's own home, we would inevitably have conversations that extended further than merely discussing CF and its treatments. Would this be crossing boundaries? I have no idea, but it was an essential part of getting to know the patients and their families and I believe that anyone working in the field of CF would agree with this.

The issue of boundary crossing becomes more ambiguous when it involves being invited to weddings, twenty-first birthday parties and even university graduations. I actually believe it was a great honour to be included in these events and it illustrates the depth of the relationship between the patient and the CF team. In the early days of my involvement in CF, I did attend many such occasions - they were usually poignant and emotional events and I remember them all very well.

~ ... ~

Liz was a young patient who was extremely unwell and was on the active lung transplant list. She was inspirational in that she lived her life to the full and always looked forward, never back. She lived in a rural cottage in north-east Scotland, with the love of her life, Luke. The cottage was fairly primitive, had little heating and was very simple. Liz had studied art at university, she loved animals and she was always kept company by her two dogs, three cats and a number of chickens roaming free in the garden. She also had a beloved horse that was kept in a field nearby. She had many friends, most of whom lived the same type of bohemian lifestyle as she did.

Liz's CF was deteriorating fast and her quality of life was becoming severely compromised. She'd had to give up her job as a charity worker and she spent more and more time at home curled up in front of the fire. Luke was a huge support - a quiet, but strong, presence and he would do anything for her; it was very moving to witness their love. In time, Liz needed to spend more and more time in hospital, requiring high-dose, long-term intravenous antibiotics and intensive physiotherapy. No matter how dire her prognosis, Liz kept her spirits up and maintained her sense of humour. It was always a pleasure to spend time on the ward with her. We had long talks about books and music, and her evident love for life and for Luke shone through, despite adversity.

As Liz's health continued to deteriorate, she and Luke decided to marry. Although neither of them had a great faith, they had befriended the hospital chaplain and he agreed to marry them. It was not clear whether Liz would be well enough to leave her hospital bed for the ceremony and contingency plans were made, just in case. The CF team were all involved with the wedding plans; we needed to ensure that, if Liz was going to leave the hospital for the day, she had enough medication and oxygen, and that she would be generally strong enough to manage the ordeal. A wheelchair was ordered and portable oxygen was delivered for her. Her medication regime was altered to enable Liz to have a few hours free of the intravenous infusion delivering her continuous antibiotics. Everyone was involved in the mission to allow Liz to have a wedding day away from the ward - from the nurses, to the consultants, to the domestic staff. It was the talk of the respiratory department and everyone hoped beyond hope that Liz would be well enough to enjoy her special day.

The entire team was invited to the wedding - but here is the dilemma: should we have accepted the invitation? Is this crossing the boundaries so clearly set out in our Code of Conduct? Are we there as her friends or as health professionals? Do we enjoy a glass of champagne to celebrate the occasion?

Looking back now, I see that we should have asked ourselves these questions at the time. Towards the end of my career, we became much stricter as a team and usually declined such invitations (and there were many), but in those early days, we tended to accept them. Many of the team did attend Liz's wedding and it was a wonderful, poignant and moving occasion. She was even able to arrive at the venue on horseback, looking like an ethereal and fragile woodland nymph coming out of the mist. Her oxygen cylinder was attached to her back and she was pale and weak, but she looked so happy. I will never forget that day and I do not regret going to the wedding. The whole team felt the same and although we enjoyed ourselves immensely, we remained professional and aware of our positions throughout the day.

~ ... ~

Another example of my involvement at a patient's wedding was perhaps clearer cut, although it still could be perceived that boundaries had been crossed. Mia was a young, vivacious woman who, although very sick, had always made the most of every moment. She was stunningly beautiful and a high achiever, having moved to work for a company in Australia a few years earlier. She was back in Scotland for a few weeks prior to getting married at a picturesque Scottish castle in the glens of Aberdeenshire. Not long after she arrived back from Australia, she needed to be admitted to the respiratory ward. She had acquired a nasty chest infection and her diabetes was uncontrolled. She had lost a great deal of weight and was severely dehydrated. It appeared that the long flight back from Australia had proved too much for her. Mia remained in hospital for the two weeks prior to her wedding, which was stressful and frustrating for her as she had so much to plan and prepare for her big day. Her condition was improving, but she was still far from her optimum health. She was discharged the day before her wedding, feeling weak but excited. Her friends and family had rallied and had relieved her of the many wedding preparations she had been so looking forward to being involved with. The CF team and ward staff lined up to wish her good luck for the special day and she left the hospital to begin her new married life.

At about 9.30 am on the day of the wedding, I got a phone call at home from her distraught father (I still do not know how he obtained my number). He told me that Mia was extremely unwell, was very breathless and had been vomiting all night. I knew that the wedding ceremony was due to start at midday and that we needed to do everything we possibly could to enable it to go ahead. My first thought was that she would be dehydrated from vomiting and if we could manage to rehydrate her, this would be a good start, if only to get her through the next few hours. She was still on her intravenous antibiotics for her infection, so they would continue as prescribed.

I phoned one of the CF consultants, who was in agreement that we should try and rehydrate Mia. Her father agreed to drive from the wedding venue to the hospital to pick up the necessary equipment required for the rehydration mission. He had a list of items required scribbled on a scrap of paper and the ward was notified that he was on his way. In the meantime, I headed from home down to the castle and arrived at the same time as her father, who was armed with saline fluid bags, lines to administer them and the necessary needles and syringes to access her port (a small indwelling device used for intravenous access).

It felt very surreal as I entered this magical castle adorned with fairy lights and flowers and ascended the stairs to the honeymoon suite. When I entered the room, there was chaos all around. There were so many people in the room, from the bridesmaids to the photographer, to the hairdresser to the make-up lady. It actually was a wonderful sight - this wedding was going ahead no matter what!

In the midst of it all, looking tiny and fragile on the huge four poster bed was Mia. She was smiling but obviously felt dreadful. I was able to get her hooked up to the intravenous infusion without any issues and soon the saline was running freely into her veins giving her a new lease of life. It never ceases to amaze me how quickly fluids can revive someone when they are dehydrated. The photographer was flitting around like a butterfly, taking pictures continuously - I wondered if he had ever seen a bride looking so unwell - and he did not seem at all perturbed by the medical activities going on. In fact, I was fairly invisible to everyone; the bride was improving, her mother had stopped crying, champagne started to flow and the mood had generally lifted. The bridesmaids were getting dressed, make-up was being put away and the hairdressers were adding the last touches to their creations. Everyone was looking and feeling merry. Once the infusion had been completed, I packed everything away and felt delighted at how much better Mia was looking and feeling. I warned her that this might just be temporary and that it was probably also the adrenaline that was helping her. I advised her not to eat too much or drink any alcohol, but otherwise just go and enjoy the day.

By this time, there was twenty minutes to go before the ceremony was due to start. I slipped away and decided that it might be prudent for me to sit at the back of the small chapel that was within the castle grounds, just to ensure she got through the ceremony without any disasters. It was already full with Mia's family and friends but I sat on the back pew near the aisle. Cameron, her husband-to-be, was sitting nervously at the front of the chapel - to this day I am unsure if he was aware at the time of the earlier dramas that had so nearly left Mia unable to attend her own wedding. The time crept on and there was no sign of Mia. We all know that it is fashionable for a bride to be late - but this late? After thirty-five minutes, I was on the brink of going to investigate when Mia and her father arrived, followed by the posse of bridesmaids. The look of relief on Cameron's face was palpable. Mia looked incredibly beautiful, but her fragility and ill health was obvious for all to see. She was just able to walk down the aisle, but needed a chair as soon as she reached Cameron. Her wedding vows were barely audible, but she managed to say them with enormous effort. It was an emotional and unforgettable occasion.

Following the ceremony, I left the castle and made my way home. Mia had kept going and was determined to enjoy the reception. Later on that evening she could manage no more and was readmitted to the ward for further rehydration and treatment. Her wedding guests continued to enjoy her wedding day back at the castle and partied into the small hours of the night - at Mia's insistence.

Had boundaries been crossed that day? Was it the right thing to do - to go to the castle and administer the saline infusion? I was undoubtedly there as a 'nurse' that day and fortunately all went well; but what if something had gone wrong? Where would I stand professionally? I had spoken with one of the consultants and she had given me the go-ahead to help Mia, but it was my ultimate responsibility to ensure the right treatment was administered in the correct way. There was no back up emergency equipment should things not have gone to plan. But the alternative would have been to call for an ambulance and to admit Mia to the hospital. She would have missed her wedding ceremony.

I had known Mia for many years; I knew her condition and I knew what she needed to help her. In most other areas of healthcare, it would not even have been a consideration to arrive at a wedding venue and administer intravenous fluids to the bride, hours before she takes her vows, but CF is different and we are frequently put into unique situations. We are often faced with extreme ethical dilemmas and we have to trust ourselves to choose the right path of action at that particular moment. I did what I thought was right at the time; Mia was able to get to her wedding and given the same situation again, I would not have done anything differently.

~ ... ~

Several years before I retired, another patient invited the whole CF team to her wedding. This particular patient had always been a difficult character. She was unpredictable, often rude and was not particularly popular amongst the team. In fact, we were all surprised to get an invitation to her wedding. It was kind of her to think of us, but in truth no one was keen to attend. This made us think about our previous behaviour when it came to such invitations. Did we only accept invitations from patients that we 'liked'? Did we make excuses when we did not want to attend a particular function? Was this the correct way to behave? Surely, we should either go to everything or we should refuse all invitations.

We all do this in our everyday lives - we ourselves decide which parties we would like to go to usually on the basis of how friendly we are with the hosts. However, as a team, we decided it was not ethical to do this with patients. We needed to treat all patients equally and, therefore, we came to the decision that we should stop accepting invitations to any social events from the CF patients, no matter how close we were to them or how long we had known them. The issue of boundaries was becoming more pertinent within the entire NHS (the advent of social media was fuelling this) and after much discussion between ourselves and management, it was decided that this was the right course of action. We were not prepared for the offence that this caused. It made me realise that our CF population definitely looked upon the team as more than just health professionals; many of them do, without doubt, think of us as friends and in some cases, we are considered part of their extended families too. It is a great privilege to be thought of in this way and again, it demonstrates the unique relationship between the CF team and the patients. However, it can also lead to potentially difficult situations and the concept of possibly crossing professional boundaries must always remain uppermost in our minds.

7
~ Burden of treatment ~

In all chronic conditions, there will be a burden of treatment. People who have diabetes will need to monitor their blood sugar levels, adjust their medication accordingly or inject themselves with insulin two or three times each day. People with high blood pressure or heart conditions will have to take regular medication and perhaps modify their diet. In CF, things are no different; except the burden of treatment is immense. CF is a complex multisystem disorder, which means that more than one treatment is needed for each of the issues. Ask anyone with CF and I would guess that one of the biggest and most difficult issues in managing their condition is trying to fit all their medications and treatments into a normal day. This is on top of trying to lead a well-balanced life with a job, school or university work, as well as maintaining healthy and happy relationships. I defy anyone to say it is possible to do this one hundred percent of the time.

If you were to meet somebody with CF in the street, the likelihood is that they would look perfectly healthy - maybe a little thin or sometimes they may be coughing - but generally they would look as healthy as the next person. What you would not realise is the amount of treatment and medication that person would need to take in order to look that way, or the time that has to be spent to lead as normal a life as possible. If any of these treatments were to be missed for any period of time, there soon would be unwanted consequences.

From a very young age, most children with CF will be required to take pancreatic enzymes to digest their food. Sometimes ten to twenty capsules are needed for each meal and it never ceases to amaze me watching these young children put a handful of capsules into their mouths and swallow them down in one go! As one patient recently said: *'this is because I have an exceptional epiglottis'*. I obviously do not have an exceptional epiglottis, as I have trouble even swallowing just one paracetamol. If pancreatic enzymes are missed for any reason, the person with CF would quickly develop severe stomach cramps, diarrhoea and would lose weight extremely quickly. Needless to say, due to these nasty, unwanted and immediate symptoms, it is one of the medications that is usually taken, even when others are missed.

As well as enzyme therapy, people with CF will usually need to take an oral long-term antibiotic, a nebulised long-term antibiotic, mucus thinning medications, vitamin tablets, steroids, antacid medications, preparations to prevent constipation, liver tablets ... the list goes on and on.

On top of these routine everyday medicines, physiotherapy is a vital part of CF treatment. This can take up to one hour, two to three times per day. And if there is an acute chest infection on top of all of this, then intravenous antibiotics may be added to the mix. These are usually strong, high dose medications taken three times a day for at least two weeks.

Patients have often told me that doing their CF treatments properly can take up to four to five hours in the day. No wonder some of these treatments get missed from time to time (or even more regularly, depending on the patient). Adherence to treatment is a major issue in CF. It is known that on average only fifty percent of daily medication is taken (this can range from thirty-five to seventy-five percent). Adherence will decline during the adolescent years and research has shown that the lowest adherence rate in CF is with young adults. If a person with CF is persistently non-adherent with their treatment, their condition will inevitably deteriorate. They will develop chest infections, often requiring hospitalisation, they will start to lose weight and their lung function will reduce. Non adherence will, without doubt, have a negative impact on a person with CF's long-term health and prognosis.

For health professionals, this is a significant issue in our day to day work. It is distressing for us to see a patient's health deteriorate, purely because they are not taking their prescribed medications. But we are the very people who have placed such a burden on these patients. What can and should we do about this?

Firstly, as health professionals, we should look at what we are actually asking the patient to take each day. Are all the medications necessary? Are we duplicating them? Are we checking exactly what a patient is taking each day before adding further treatments? Maybe the patient is not taking the tablets because of the side effects - are we asking about these? Once we have ensured all of the above, should we then try and talk to the patient about possible reasons for the non-adherence and to help look for solutions to this problem?

We rely on the patient being honest and open with us. I know of many occasions when a patient has told us what we want to hear: *'Yes, I have been taking my nebuliser each day'*; *'I haven't missed a single dose of my IV course'; 'I always take my enzymes, I would never miss any'*. Sometimes, a patient tells the pharmacist they are diligently taking everything and in the next half hour tells the nurses they have missed a week of their antibiotics. Do they not realise we speak to each other?

Over the years, we get to know which are the patients who always take their intravenous medications come rain or shine; we also know those who are prone to missing a few treatments here and there and, finally, we know of the patients who are very 'non-adherent individuals'. This latter group may be the lovable rogues, the disgruntled adolescent, the person who is going through a tough time in their personal lives, or it may simply be down to personality. There will be many different reasons for non-adherence and as health professionals, we are there to try to help with this issue.

I have been on many committees and groups working on solutions to the issue of non-adherence in CF and I have come to the conclusion that there is no easy answer. In fact, I do not believe that an answer exists. It is human nature to not always conform or comply with rules and regulations and people with CF are no different when it comes to their treatments.

There are some things, however, that we can do to help. It is imperative that the patient knows *why* we have asked them to take any particular treatment. *How* it will help, *what* mechanism it has in the body, *what* side effects it may have and *what* might happen if the medication is missed. As health professionals, we need to foster an honest and non-judgemental relationship between ourselves and the patient, and if this is well established, it is more likely that you will hear the truth as to what the patient is doing or not doing regarding their treatments.

We also need to establish the reason for why the patient might not be taking their tablets. Is there something going on at school? Is there a timing issue in the mornings? Is there something else more significant going on? I can recall one young teenager in particular who was so clinically depressed that she decided to stop taking all her medication in order to purposefully become unwell. It was incredible how quickly she lost weight, how fast her lung function declined and how chesty she became. It was certainly a cry for help and she would say that she was actually attempting to commit a slow suicide.

There has been a lot of research done that has shown that patients with CF generally get better more quickly when they are admitted to hospital. This is largely because in hospital they are forced to rest, they get all their medications in a timely manner and they see members of the CF team on a daily basis - this enables them to get regular physiotherapy and dietetic reviews. Blood samples will be taken, which will show either an improvement, or otherwise, in their infection markers, leading to the antibiotic regime being altered as necessary. Patients with CF will always get a single room on the ward, due to infection control issues and often their rooms will become social gathering places for their families, friends and ward nurses. Conversely, patients may lose weight while in hospital, due to the well documented issue of hospital meals. Hospital catering departments are faced with an incredibly difficult dilemma: they receive a pitiful amount of money for each patient and, with this daily allowance, they have to produce a good quality meal that is healthy, nutritious and value for money - an almost impossible task. To overcome this problem, families and friends usually supplement the hospital meal with all sorts of goodies and treats - encouraged by the dietician, as gaining and maintaining weight is a vital component in the treatment of CF.

Although it is known that CF patients generally do better following a hospital stay, imagine requiring a two-week hospital admission for intravenous antibiotics every couple of months or so? What an upheaval to daily life. For patients trying to hold down employment, look after a family, attend school or university, this is a major intrusion into the rigid routine that many of them have developed over the years. Although the ward nurses try to make the hospital admissions as pleasant as possible for the patients, it is not generally fun or psychologically stimulating to be in hospital. Many of the young patients leave the ward during the afternoons (usually with permission, although not always) and sometimes do not return until minutes before their evening dose of antibiotics is due. On one occasion, a young girl even went on to a nightclub, after going to the cinema, one evening and returned to the ward very much the worse for wear. Needless to say, despite feeling dreadful the following day, she was severely spoken to by members of the CF team.

Examples such as this exacerbate the frustration and despair felt by some of the ward staff and management. Hospital admissions are very precious; there is always a shortage of beds and usually patients are discharged at the earliest possible opportunity to enable the next patient to occupy the space. Patients with CF are often seen as taking advantage of their admissions by treating the ward as a 'hotel' rather than a place of rest and recovery. As a team, we had to become strict with ward rules, especially for the younger patients and we even drew up a 'contract' of acceptable behaviour expected during an admission. However, it is also important to see things from the side of the patient. Very often, a young adolescent will their CF, hate hospital admissions and will have far more important things to be getting on with outside of the hospital. Are they ever going to be the 'perfect patient'?

To diminish the burden of hospital admissions (and to relieve the pressure on acute beds in the wards), many patients are taught to administer their own courses of intravenous antibiotics at home. This will reduce the number of days they need to be in hospital and will enable them to continue leading as normal a life as possible. It is not a simple procedure to teach a patient (or sometimes their carers) to take on the responsibility of administering their own antibiotics. There are many issues to consider, including the chance of a reaction to the medication (worst case scenario being anaphylactic shock). Is the patient or carer capable of doing this, are the home conditions conducive to storing and giving such drugs? It is a significant undertaking for the patient and carer, as well as for us. If anything were to go wrong, it would ultimately be our responsibility.

Before enabling anyone to self-administer intravenous antibiotics at home, we always did a risk assessment in the patient's house to ensure that they were capable and confident in carrying out such a technical and responsible procedure. We also endeavoured to do an annual assessment of intravenous administration to ensure technique and storage arrangements were satisfactory, although I have to admit this was difficult to fulfil one hundred percent of the time due to staff shortages, lack of resources and general patient demand. However, knowing the patients as we did, it was usually clear to us who would manage this and who would find it difficult.

~ ... ~

We visited one particular patient on a regular basis. Ali lived in a small, cramped three-bed council flat which was shared with her parents, older brother and his young son. There was no spare space, with toys strewn around the floor, laundry hanging over chairs and radiators, and food and dirty plates covering every surface in the kitchen. It was a chaotic home in difficult circumstances. On one particular occasion, things appeared worse than ever. Ali's CF equipment was all over the place. Her vast quantities of medications shared a cupboard in the kitchen with tins of beans and packets of crisps; her boxes of needles and syringes were piled high on a table in the sitting room. Her bins for collecting used needles were also in a precarious pile on the floor. Some of these storage situations were inevitable and they would have been acceptable, as long as they were out of reach of the young child also living in the home and kept away from extreme heat, cold or damp. However, these bins full of needles and other sharp items just perched on top of each other were not acceptable. They were within easy reach of the child, some of the lids were not put on properly and they could have toppled over at the slightest nudge. This sent alarm signals out to me - the issue was not only that it was a dangerous situation but also, why did Ali think this was OK? Was she aware of the dangers that these bins posed to her nephew?

I had always been keen that Ali should be allowed to administer her intravenous antibiotics at home. She was unwell and her condition was deteriorating fast. She had many personal issues and she found hospital admissions difficult. Her family found it hard to visit regularly, as they lived three bus journeys away and both parents had jobs with unsociable hours. I thought that over the years, Ali had matured into a sensible and mostly conscientious young woman and she had assured me that she was capable of taking on this responsibility. Certainly, when observing her making up her medication, using the needles and syringes to draw up and dilute her antibiotics and finally administering it through her port, she appeared proficient and capable. She knew how to store everything in principle, she was aware of potential risks and infection hazards. Her mother was willing to support her in this and we would be offering regular visits and contact.

So, I was dismayed to see the general chaos that surrounded Ali on this occasion. When I looked in her kitchen cupboards, I found hordes of boxes of half used courses of antibiotics, steroid tablets and other medications. It was obvious that she had been struggling to cope with her treatments, but had not mentioned anything to us. As a team, we had no choice but to remove the opportunity of her doing her own intravenous antibiotics at home. She was devastated and pleaded with us, saying she would change and manage it all in future. But we could not give in; it was too big a responsibility from both sides and we could not take any risks. As a result, Ali required several long-term hospital admissions for intravenous antibiotics and general CF care. It was not easy from both sides and it definitely jeopardised our relationship with her for a while, but her condition did improve and we knew that she was getting all her treatment as prescribed.

Ali died a year or so after this. She had a massive haemoptysis (bleeding from the lungs). It was a distressing and traumatic way to die, but she was in her own bed at home when it happened and I hope very much that she was not aware of what was happening. She had always said that she wanted to die in her own bed when the time came, and I know this was a small comfort to her parents in the months that followed.

~ ... ~

Ali's situation is one of so many examples that illustrates the pressure and frustration that can be caused by the burden of treatment for people with CF. There is no easy answer to this, but with the advent of new modulator medicines that are in the pipeline, it may be that some of these issues may be resolved in the future. However, non-adherence, rebellion and pure forgetfulness is part of human nature, and this should never be overlooked or forgotten.

8
~ Infection control ~

The general public will have had some experience of infection control issues over recent years, following health scares with pathogens such as MARS, SERS, swine flu and the more recent unprecedented event of the Covid-19 coronavirus, which has caused so much upheaval in all of our lives. This will have given some insight into some of the problems that people with CF have to face every day of their lives with regards to infection. The worry of catching the bug, passing it to someone else who may be susceptible, the issue of constant and thorough handwashing and just being too near others who are coughing and sneezing. Bacteria and viruses are continually mutating and changing, causing novel and unknown pathogens to emerge from time to time throughout the world. For most, these health scares are temporary and will pass, allowing everyone to get on with their normal lives again, but for others, the impact of catching such an infection may be long lasting or even fatal.

Infection control is obviously pertinent to all clinical situations in any health setting, especially a hospital, but in CF the implications of poor infection control are devastating.

It may be helpful to describe some of the pathological (disease causing) bacteria that can be harmful to the CF lung. However, it is important to point out that the bacteria mentioned below do not usually cause any harm to people with healthy lungs. These bacteria are more prevalent at certain ages and in certain environments in people with CF. Babies with CF are usually born with near normal lungs, infection free. Due to the moist, thick and sticky environment in the lungs of a person with CF, bacteria and other pathogens thrive and may quickly establish themselves within this compatible host. I often used the analogy that the bugs thought of the lungs as a warm and welcoming 'compost heap' - a perfect environment for multiplying and setting up home. Once bacteria became established within the lungs, it could be very difficult to eradicate them. They inhabited the lungs on a full-time basis and would flare up from time to time, causing an acute lung infection, which would need to be treated with antibiotics - either intravenous, nebulised or oral. These antibiotics would subdue the exacerbation and reduce the inflammation within the lungs, but may not eradicate the bacteria altogether. As a result, the lungs would be slightly more damaged and scarred with each acute infection, in turn creating an even more conducive environment in which the bacteria could thrive.

The next section of this chapter is going to use some fairly long and unpronounceable spelling for various types of bacteria and other pathogens found within the 'CF lung'. These names do not need to be learned or remembered, but it is important for the understanding of the complexity of cross infection issues. So, here goes ...

A young child with CF would often culture fairly innocuous bacteria in their sputum, such as *Staphylococcus aureus* or *Haemophilus influenzae*. These bugs can be easily treated with oral antibiotics and generally do not cause too much trouble. Some people with CF only ever culture *Staphylococcus aureus* and never seem to move onto the more serious bacterial growths; this may be dependent on their genotype (CF gene mutation) or the environment in which they live.

Often, during the adolescent phase, another more serious bacteria may manifest within the lungs. This beast is called *Pseudomonas aeruginosa* and was the bug that all people with CF dreaded getting. When I first started working in CF this was the most serious type of infection, but over the years, things have changed and there are now more sinister infections that patients hope to avoid. *Pseudomonas aeruginosa* is a common environmental pathogen, found in kitchens, bathrooms, hot tubs and sinks. It is the green slimy growth found on cut flowers when they have been left in the vase too long - anyone who has removed such stems from stagnant water will recognise the familiar smell of decaying plants - this is *pseudomonas*. It is known to be an 'opportunistic' bacterium, meaning it will only manifest itself in people who already have CF, or another condition that weakens the body's immune system. People who have perfectly healthy lungs are unlikely to catch a *pseudomonas* chest infection. Research has shown that people with CF who are colonised with *Pseudomonas aeruginosa* will have a significantly shorter life expectancy than those who are only colonised with *Staphylococcus aureus* or those who grow neither of these bugs.

There are only one or two oral antibiotics that are effective against *Pseudomonas aeruginosa* and usually infections need to be treated with either nebulised or intravenous antibiotics. Occasionally the bacteria can be eradicated if it is treated appropriately and early, but more often, once it has established itself, it becomes colonised within the lungs and is difficult to get rid of. Some people with CF will manage quite happily over the years culturing regular *Pseudomonas aeruginosa* in their sputum, only requiring occasional antibiotics, whereas others will find it much more troublesome and detrimental to their health. There is no rhyme or reason as to how it will affect different people, but good adherence to a medication regime will, without doubt, be beneficial.

After I had been working in CF for several years, another bug, called *Burkholderia cepacia,* raised its head. Little was known initially in CF about this bacterium when it first emerged. *Cepacia* was first identified as "onion rot" in the 1940's - the black slimy substance found on onions as they started to decay - and the first time it was described as a human pathogen was in the 1950's. It is known to be another environmental bacterium found also in water and soil. In the 1980's and 1990's, it began to appear as a pathogen in CF, with some strains of *cepacia* seeming to be extremely infectious. Up until this time, there was encouragement for people with CF to engage with each other, have holidays together (several charities ran CF holidays which included lots of group activities) and exercise together. It was after several people with CF in an exercise class in a regional CF centre seemed to culture the same strain of *cepacia* that it was realised that perhaps it was not a good idea to encourage this type of interaction after all.

Gradually, over the next few years, all CF centres started to segregate patients from each other. From a psychological perspective, this was a difficult thing to do for the patients. They really enjoyed meeting and chatting with each other and often the clinic waiting room was a hive of social activity. Those who had been on the CF holidays together were especially close and shared many happy memories. But we had no choice; this virulent bug was causing havoc in some of the CF community. It caused acute and severe chest infections, which were proving difficult to treat. It appeared to be resistant to most of the routine antibiotics that we used in CF. Throughout the world it was being reported that some patients had succumbed to a quick and traumatic death soon after acquiring cepacia - subsequently known as '*cepacia* syndrome'.

~ ... ~

Anna was a delightful young patient whom we looked after. She was in her early twenty's and life was good. She was bubbly and vivacious and her CF was under control. She had a new boyfriend and had recently started a job following her university years. She was one of the patients that it was a pleasure to see emerging from her teenage years and maturing into a resilient, resourceful, intelligent and humorous young woman. When she first cultured *cepacia* in her sputum, I clearly remember having to break the news to her. We did not have much experience with the bug at this time, but we knew it was a nasty bacterium to have and that we needed to do everything to try and eradicate it. Anna and her parents were devastated. They had read newspaper articles about *cepacia* and they were in touch with others in the CF community. The power of the internet was emerging and there were all sorts of horror stories written about patients all over the world who had suffered from this particular bacterium. It was hard to offer reassurance when we were not sure what we were dealing with, and we too had heard many of the negative accounts. Anna was treated aggressively with a strong cocktail of intravenous antibiotics and for a few months, it seemed that her body was coping with this new inhabitant. She was enjoying her new job and was feeling energetic and well.

One morning, as I arrived at work, I heard that Anna had been admitted as an emergency to the respiratory ward overnight. She had an acute infection and was extremely unwell. I was shocked when I saw her - she was pale, breathless and was in obvious discomfort. She was also very scared. She was hooked up to various monitors, tubes were being inserted into her veins and she was on a multitude of drugs. But things were deteriorating. Over the next few days, the decision was made to move her to the intensive care unit.

Her devoted parents were distraught; to see their beautiful young daughter struggling like this must have been beyond their worst nightmares. No one can imagine what parents must go through at a time like this. I could only offer my support and presence, while the intensive care team did their jobs in providing the best care that Anna could have received at this traumatic time. It is at times like this that as a nurse, you become incredibly close to people as they go through the worst times of their lives. I spent hours with Anna's parents over the next couple of weeks, sitting in the stark, airless relatives' room or by her bedside in the intensive care unit. Offering cups of tea, a shoulder to cry on, a listening ear. Relatives will often feel very helpless, especially parents watching their child suffering. The role of a parent is seen to be helping and 'fixing' problems and issues for their children - it must be so painful to have to stand back and watch things get worse and worse without being able to do anything. If it is of any comfort, just 'being there' is probably doing more than any parent or carer will ever know. It has been shown again and again that the last sense to leave a person is the sense of hearing and I am sure that just by being close, holding a hand or whispering words of love helps patients in their last hours.

Anna finally reached the time when major decisions had to be made. She was diagnosed as having '*cepacia* syndrome', a new and, at that time, fairly unknown phenomenon that had been described elsewhere with other CF patients in various parts of the world. Three weeks earlier, Anna had been well, was working full time and was enjoying life to the full. Nobody in their wildest dreams could have envisaged what was to ensue over the next month. Her life support was switched off and Anna died peacefully in the intensive care unit with her family beside her. The *cepacia* had engulfed her body and she was unable to cope with this virulent and aggressive bacterium. It was terribly tragic and one of the CF deaths that will stay with me forever.

~ ... ~

Although we had other patients who seemed to manage well whilst culturing *cepacia*, Anna's death made us realise the devastating impact it could have, and we rapidly instigated a 'segregation' policy for all of the patients. Everything had to be done to prevent the spread of this bug. Although it was not precisely known how the infection occurred, there was growing evidence that person to person spread was likely, for example through coughing and sharing cutlery. Those who were already culturing *cepacia* were asked to attend a specific clinic held on the first Thursday of each month and no patients were permitted to socialise together in the clinic waiting room. Patients went to individual rooms as soon as they arrived in the clinic and did not leave the room until their appointment was over.

Today, this is a well-established and accepted way of running CF clinics all over the world, but in those days it was difficult. Patients felt stigmatised and strongly objected to being separated from their friends, many of whom had known each other for years.

Cross infection procedures and protocols in hospitals have become more stringent over the years (not only in CF), for very good reasons. As various bacteria and other pathogens become more virulent and resistant to treatment, it is imperative that everything is done to prevent any risk of cross infection. Good education and communication are key between all health professionals working in CF, whether in the clinic, ward or community situation. Patients and their families are nowadays generally understanding and accepting of the situation, but it does not make it any easier for them.

Unfortunately, over the last decade or so, another nasty bacterium has emerged, known as *Mycobacterium abscessus* (a relative of, but not the same, as the better-known *Mycobacterium tuberculosis* or TB). In the same way that *cepacia* is resistant to many of the common antibiotics, *Mycobacterium abscessus* is also fiercely difficult to treat. It will often require a long-term course of strong, sometimes toxic antibiotics, starting with at least one month's course of intravenous antibiotics (which usually needed to be given in hospital). As more is being discovered about *Mycobacterium abscessus*, it appears that cross infection may occur from person to person, although it is also found in the environment, especially in wet and warm places such as sinks and showers. One difference from some of the other bacterial pathogens is that it seems to survive much longer outside of the host and it is difficult to 'kill'. This has created further anxiety regarding segregation, as patients who are culturing *Mycobacterium abscessus* now need to be seen in rooms away from the general clinic, because it cannot be guaranteed that they have been fully decontaminated between patients. One particular CF centre in Scotland is actually seeing patients colonised with *Mycobacterium abscessus* in an entirely different hospital.

The most significant outcome for a patient with CF becoming colonised with *Mycobacterium abscessus* is that it will exclude them from lung transplantation. This is because the transplant centre used by Scotland has said (at the current time) that having *abscessus* is an 'absolute' contraindication to transplant. This is also the case for most other centres in the UK, although some say it is only a 'relative' contraindication. There have been some disastrous outcomes following transplant in such patients, with most patients succumbing to horrendous infection following the operation leading to a rapid and traumatic death. It is devastating news for a patient to hear that they are no longer eligible for lung transplantation, although it does make the decision to undergo the gruelling long-term *abscessus* eradication treatment a little easier for them.

As with any new and emerging complication, there is much debate and discussion regarding the best way to deal with this bacterium. I was on a Scottish working group committee, formed to look at this very issue, which ultimately had to be disbanded, due to differing views and some very strong opinions on this topic; however, as further research is done and more robust evidence is shown, it will become easier to streamline the infection control policies and procedures throughout the UK.

One difficult scenario regarding infection control is that of siblings or close relatives with CF, who each culture different bacteria within their lungs. There is no easy solution to advising against cross infection in this situation, but surprisingly there have been many examples of such siblings living together and sharing the same lifestyle but still not infecting each other with each other's bugs.

~ ... ~

Andrew and Karen were a brother and sister who both had CF. They came from a close and loving family who lived in a small rural community about twenty miles from the CF unit.

Karen was the elder of the siblings by two years and had always kept better health than Andrew. She looked more robust and she did not seem to be affected by many of the CF issues that Andrew endured, such as diabetes and liver disease. She got through university without any problems, settled down to a full-time job and moved out to live independently. It always interested me that two siblings, with the same CF genotype and who grew up together in the same home could manifest their CF in such different ways. It dispelled the idea that living in close proximity would inevitably mean the same bacteria would be harboured in each other's lungs.

Karen married and had a son, who was the love of her life. They adored each other and Karen was the happiest she had ever been. It was lovely to see. She remained extremely close to Andrew, but I know she always had a sense of guilt in the back of her mind that she was so much healthier than her brother.

Andrew had required a lung transplant in 2009. His life prior to this had become extremely difficult. I remember visiting him at home, while he was trying to eat lunch. He was so breathless that it was impossible for him to eat, breathe and swallow at the same time. It was easier for him not to eat at all and just to concentrate on breathing. It was heart-breaking to see his mother looking so broken and feeling so helpless as she tried to persuade him to have just one more mouthful of his lunch.

However, following his transplant, Andrew's life had transformed. He was now working full-time and was leading a fulfilled and busy life; a stark contrast to the horrendously poor quality of life he was leading prior to his new lungs.

So, for Andrew, the transplant was a huge success and changed his life beyond all belief. He was able to return to leading a normal life, despite needing to take a multitude of anti-rejection drugs for the rest of his life. These particular drugs can lower resistance to infections, making those taking them especially susceptible to coughs, colds and other more serious pathogens.

We advised Karen and Andrew on the risks of cross infection following the transplant. He would, without doubt, be more prone to catching nasty chest infections and it was vital that everything was done to avoid this. They were both intelligent people who used their common sense in this respect and avoided each other if Karen had an infection. They did not spend time together in small enclosed rooms and at times such as Christmas, they sat at opposite ends of the table. At this point, Karen was culturing *Pseudomonas aeruginosa,* a bug that Andrew had also grown prior to his transplant.

Imagine all of our dismay when one of Karen's sputum cultures came back as showing a growth of *Mycobacterium abscessus.* The beast of all bacteria and one that we did not wish any of our patients to grow. We did not know how she had come across this pathogen or how it would affect her. As mentioned earlier, it is an environmental bug, often found in water - but as with most patients the source may never be identified. There was also a chance that she had acquired it by means of cross infection, either in the clinic or in the ward.

For Karen, this was a disaster. For someone who was previously very well, coping with her treatments, and who had a full, happy and contented family life. She had remained very close to Andrew, who adored his young nephew, and they spent many happy times together. Now Karen was growing *Mycobacterium abscessus*, everything changed.

We advised Karen that she should only see Andrew if absolutely necessary and not at all if she had any signs of an acute infection. They should not be together in enclosed environments and they were made highly aware of all the risks of cross infection. Because Andrew was immunosuppressed, he was at a much greater risk of catching *Mycobacterium abscessus* and for him, this would be a catastrophe. The transplant centre was even more stringent in its advice than we were, having obviously had experience of disastrous situations post-transplantation with patients who had grown this potentially terrifying bug.

The most difficult time for the family was at Christmas - their parents were torn between seeing Karen or Andrew, as they were also very aware of the cross-infection risk. As well as the practical risks of this infection, it has many psychological aspects to it as well. The stigma of knowing that you cannot see your brother in case you give him a deadly infection; the devastating news that you are no longer eligible for transplantation; the guilt that would be felt if Andrew were to have caught *Mycobacterium abscessus;* and purely the knowledge of the rigorous treatment ahead in order to attempt eradication.

It was also at this time that Karen was keen to try for another baby, but she was told that this was not advisable, mainly due to the toxic effects of the long-term antibiotic treatment she would be taking over the next few years. It was a tough time for her and I will never forget the hours of sitting with her while she was trying to come to terms with the fact that she would only have one child.

What a devastating effect this bug had on the entire family.

Karen was one of the first patients to culture *Mycobacterium abscessus* in our centre. The treatment for this was still fairly new and untested. She underwent a rigorous course of initial intravenous antibiotics, requiring a four-week admission to the ward. This was followed with a two-year course of oral and nebulised antibiotics. The combination of these drugs is strong and difficult to tolerate, often causing multiple side effects and symptoms such as nausea and dizziness. But Karen persevered. I am happy to report that the treatment did appear to be successful in her case and now, five years later, she is still free from culturing *Mycobacterium abscessus*. The family has 'reunited' and, although the threat of growing it once again is always present, Karen can continue to fully enjoy family life once more.

~ ... ~

The emergence of such bacteria as *Burkholderia cepacia* and *Mycobacterium abscessus* in CF has been an added cause of concern and anxiety to all of those living with the condition. As well as affecting patients and their families, they have also had a huge impact on the CF team and other health professionals involved with their care.

As nurses, it has changed the way we work in CF. We have to plan our workload so that we only see patients with these bugs at the end of the working day, and if we have seen a patient with *Mycobacterium abscessus* we try not to see any other patients that day. When a CF patient with *Mycobacterium abscessus* requires admission, they will often need to be admitted to a different ward from the usual respiratory ward setting, so there is no risk of people with CF coming into contact with each other or the ward staff inadvertently cross infecting patients. There are also significant implications for laboratory staff and the microbiology team; not only do they spend hours and costly resources on culturing and identifying the different pathogens, but they also decide how best to treat them and which would be the least toxic combination of antibiotics for patients.

And of course, there is the issue of antibiotic resistance and the ever-growing shortage of effective medication to use to treat such bugs. There is a desperate need for new antibiotics, not only in CF but throughout clinical medicine today.

# 9
~ A glass half full ~

One area that has always interested me in caring for anyone with a chronic condition is what impact does *personality* have in the progression of the illness? CF is no exception to this. You will, by now, be aware of the complex nature of CF and the devastating effect it can have on everyday life.

Research has shown that people with CF tend to be resilient individuals, who cope with everyday adversities, such as divorce, bereavement and moving homes, better than the general population. We can surmise that this might be because they are so used to living with a lifelong condition with major implications that 'smaller' life stresses are kept in perspective.

The majority of the patients that I cared for were diagnosed in childhood, although there were a number of patients who were found to have CF as adults. Although most of these patients had not had to cope with the shock and adjustment of receiving this diagnosis as adults, there will have been times during their lives when crises will have occurred: the progression of the disease and the addressing of certain milestones, such as transplantation or diabetes. During such times, the patient's usual routine would need to stop and be adapted, until these setbacks were addressed and were hopefully under control once again. There was a useful diagram that I occasionally used with patients showing an independence/ dependence scale and this illustrated the fact that a person may move backwards and forwards along this continuum depending on the stage of their illness.

Scale of independence

| Completely dependent | | Completely independent |

We always tried to encourage patients to be as independent and to lead as normal a life as possible. Our mantra was to *'live life with CF rather than let CF be your life - have control over CF rather than CF having control over you'*. Our ethos was to empower patients to take control over their own treatments and to contact the CF team directly, if they needed help or advice. This was vital, in order for each patient to incorporate their CF into their own lifestyles and to be able to live as normal a life as possible.

As the condition deteriorated for some of the patients, they often felt they were losing control and this could be replaced by a feeling of hopelessness and disempowerment. This was especially true when a patient needed to spend more time in hospital on intravenous antibiotics and the impact on work and social life became obvious. In these situations, it was hard to accept that CF was beginning to take over their lives, especially when having enjoyed independent living, they may need to move back home with parents, or give up work.

In such situations, people will cope differently, depending on their personality. There are many well-documented ways of coping with adversity and it is not for me to comment on which are right or wrong. As healthcare professionals, our job was to ensure that patients and their families received the best support possible at these difficult times and we tried to offer realistic hope and goals for each individual situation.

There is no doubt that personality plays a significant part in how a person will cope with a condition such as CF. Over the years I have seen how the positive 'glass half-full' patient copes with adversity, compared to someone who considers such situations as 'glass half-empty'. The research literature on optimism and pessimism is extensive and all conclusions are that it is generally more beneficial to be an optimistic person in all spheres of life, such as the workplace, academic studies, relationships and sport. Coping with illness is no different. It is difficult to 'learn' how to be more optimistic, especially if you are a naturally pessimistic person, although there are a multitude of self-help books on the market for this purpose. And, it should also be remembered that living with CF is not easy at the best of times. It takes a very special person to remain entirely optimistic and positive throughout the whole of their CF journey.

~...~

Dave was a lovable rogue. He was a good-looking, cheeky, cockney chap who had moved to the north-east of Scotland from his native Essex in the 1980's. His accent had developed into an interesting mix of estuary London and Scottish dialect over the years! Dave was never quiet, always had jokes to tell and he never sat still. He had a lot of fingers in a lot of pies, and over all the years I knew him, he never had a stable job for more than a few months at a time.

It was always a breath of fresh air to see Dave at the clinic. He was good fun and his humour was infectious. We always felt better after a 'Dave appointment'.

Dave had had a tough life. His family background was complex and his mother left the family for a new life in America when Dave was a teenager. His father remarried and moved to France, leaving Dave and his sister to fend for themselves. But Dave was a 'coper' - he did not feel sorry for himself and he did not let things get him down. Over the years, his CF became increasingly difficult to manage and he required regular hospitalisations and IV antibiotics. The ward nurses enjoyed Dave's admissions - his single room would be a social hub of entertainment and loud laughter could often be heard emanating from behind the closed door. He was not in denial about his condition - on the contrary, he was always keen to know about new treatments and how we thought his illness was progressing. We had many long and open talks about transplantation and I especially remember a poignant situation, when he was keen that I talked honestly to his young nieces and nephews about what their Uncle Dave was facing ahead of him.

The time came when Dave was put on the lung transplant list. By now, he was finding it very hard to manage day-to-day living and he was relying more and more heavily on his partner and friends. It is interesting that such positive people usually have a large and diverse group of friends, all of whom offer support and encouragement in their own ways. People generally like to be around positive people, no matter what adversity they are facing. Dave was always accompanied by a friend to the clinic (usually a different one each time) and despite finding it difficult to talk or breathe at times, he always managed to crack a joke, usually at the most inappropriate times. I will never forget the hacking cough that wracked his ribs every time he made people laugh. I think it was the most painful cough I have ever heard.

After two long years of waiting on the lung transplant list, Dave got the call for the operation. He was fast running out of time and his old lungs were almost useless. The joy felt amongst the CF team that day was palpable. We were all very fond of Dave and we so admired the way he had coped with his deteriorating illness. We remained on tenterhooks all day for news of how the procedure had gone. After what seemed like an interminable time, we got word that all had gone well and the operation had been a success. What a relief!

Although CF life post-transplant can also be gruelling, Dave continued his inbuilt positive attitude to life - although his lungs had nearly given up on him, he never gave up on his life. He is now several years from his transplant and because all is going well, he is not seen as often at the clinic. However, whenever we do see him, those 'Dave appointments' still leave us feeling like we have been hit by a whirlwind - full of fun and laughter.

And he still does not have a stable job, but who cares?

~...~

Stuart was a young boy with CF whom I first met when he was fifteen years old. He was due to transfer from the children's service to the adult service and he was extremely nervous about this move. He had highly intelligent, slightly overbearing parents and as a team, we had been pre-warned about the family and their anxiety.

Stuart was a bright boy, but he left school as soon as he could and he was isolated with few friends. During his frequent hospital admissions, I do not ever remember seeing anybody outside the family coming to visit him. He decided not to go to college or university and he felt his CF was too severe to allow him to find employment. As a result, he lived at home and spent long periods on his own, as his parents were out at work.

How severe was his CF? It was difficult to tell, as he perceived it to be very bad. It was impossible to get an accurate lung function recording as we never knew if he was trying his hardest (some of the patients spent hours repeating their lung function again and again until they beat their last reading!), but this was not the case with Stuart. One or two feeble blows into the spirometer machine, and that was it. He phoned us on a regular basis stating that he had an infection and needed antibiotics. He became obsessed with the colour, consistency and amount of his sputum and would report each episode of coughing and breathlessness in minute detail to us. Exercise and activity featured little in his day to day life and I am sure that time dragged interminably for him. He was the archetypal 'heart sink' patient.

As a team, we did everything we could think of to help him. Our psychologist became involved and tried to interest him in hobbies and easily achievable goals, but to no avail. Stuart would try something for a short while but then become disillusioned and said he found it easier to remain at home in his familiar, non-threatening surroundings. Painting, yoga, volunteering; these things all came and went, but Stuart did not persevere with any of them. And the more time he spent on his own at home, the more time he spent thinking about his CF.

His condition did start to deteriorate. This was probably inevitable, as the disease started to take its natural course. Stuart was certainly diligent in taking all his treatments; he really was one of the few patients who took all his medications at the right time all of the time. It will never be known whether he would have gone downhill as quickly, had he been more active, more positive and more motivated - we can only surmise, but without a doubt, the downwards trajectory was hard for Stuart and his family.

The time came eventually when we had to discuss lung transplantation with him. Rightly or wrongly, we had all been dreading this moment. Knowing how Stuart usually saw the negative aspect of everything, we assumed that he would react badly to this conversation. We thought his anxiety would become more heightened and it may lead to further melancholy and depression. How wrong we were ...

It was as if a shadow had been lifted for Stuart. He found it such a relief that the subject of transplant had been raised. He had known this was going to be inevitable and he had been waiting for this moment for months. The 'elephant in the room' had been addressed and he felt a weight had been lifted from his shoulders. He admitted that he had been dreading this conversation and that he had already read extensively on the subject. However, when it happened it was better than he was expecting;

there was light at the end of his very long tunnel and there was the prospect of a better future.

The CF team learnt a few things from Stuart that day. On reflection, we may have put off this usually difficult conversation for fear of Stuart's reaction. Little did we realise that he had just been waiting for it to happen and had put his life on hold for it. Why were we so apprehensive about addressing this issue with Stuart? Was it because his expected reaction would make us feel uncomfortable? Or was it because we did not want to cause Stuart himself more discomfort and reason to despair?

Although we had a small glimpse into Stuart's innermost thoughts and we saw a change in his demeanour that day, his personality did not significantly change as a result of this conversation. A few months later, he questioned whether he actually wanted a lung transplant after all. He did not like the sound of the possible complications after the operation and he became squeamish at the idea of having someone else's lungs inside his body. His biggest fear was that the surgeon would drop the new lungs onto the floor by mistake, leaving him with no lungs, and therefore certain death. I remember spending many hours with him discussing the pros and cons of transplant and we never came to any satisfactory conclusions.

Stuart did end up having a lung transplant - he was a straightforward candidate for the operation, in that he did not have any of the contraindications that can make the procedure so difficult. On paper, one would have expected him to make a routine, uncomplicated recovery but this did not happen. Stuart spent many weeks at the transplant centre whilst he tried to come to terms with his new lungs. He was reluctant to exercise, he stopped eating and he felt very fragile for a long time. After two months, he returned home and he slowly began to embrace this wonderful gift he had been given.

Stuart did have several years of good health - his lungs served him well and he was given new opportunities that other people would have jumped at the chance of doing. However, as the saying goes: *'a leopard doesn't change its spots'* - Stuart did try going to university, he did get a kitten and he even moved out to live independently for a while.

But none of this lasted. He found university too stressful, the kitten grew into a cat and he found it easier to live at home.

~ ... ~

To compare Dave and Stuart is to compare chalk and cheese. Two different people with the same condition, but with totally different attitudes to life. If asked, Dave would probably say that he has had a good life and has made the most of his opportunities. Stuart may well say the same about his life. Who are we to say who is right? Certainly, one of these two was 'easier' for us to look after than the other, but we do not choose the personality we are born with (although some may argue this), just as someone does not choose to be born with CF.

10
~ Ali's story ~

Ali has already been introduced to you earlier in the book and I want to revisit her and share more of her story. She was the young lady who found it difficult to manage her intravenous treatment in her chaotic home, and eventually we had to stop her from doing this.

I knew Ali from the age of fourteen. When Ali was this age, she was a boy. Her name at that point was Alistair and he was similar to many of our other teenage patients in that he missed multiple clinic appointments, was erratic in taking his medications and did not engage us in any form of conversation. He dressed as a 'goth', usually wearing all black with black makeup and nails. He loved music and he always brightened up and became more animated when this subject was discussed. His CF was fairly mild at this stage, which was fortunate for him, considering his lack of adherence to treatments.

Alistair lived in a small rented flat in a tough area of town. His parents were a hardworking couple - at one point his mother had three simultaneous jobs, just to make ends meet. She would occasionally accompany him to his clinic appointments, braving the elements as they caught the three buses needed to get to the hospital. His mother tried hard to keep on top of Alistair's treatments, but she was simply a very busy lady and I am not sure she fully understood the significance of his CF. She often sat in the clinic looking like a scared rabbit in the headlights, and she rarely asked questions or showed any great interest in his condition. They would escape from the clinic as soon as they could and we would rarely hear anything from them until Alistair was next due to be seen.

Over the years, we got to know Alistair better. He was an interesting chap, with deep thoughts and an artistic mind. He only ever mentioned one friend to us - someone who lived close by and had similar interests to himself.

When Alistair was in his early twenties, he developed CF-related diabetes. About half of people with CF will eventually develop diabetes - due to the pancreas becoming shrivelled and scarred, thus not able to produce insulin normally. 'CF-related diabetes' is not the same as either Type I or Type II diabetes and it is treated in a different way. Injections of insulin may be instigated quickly and the diet will not be altered. In CF, due to the propensity to lose weight because of malabsorption, it is important that a high-calorie, high-carbohydrate diet is maintained. This differs from the treatment of other types of diabetes. Conflicting advice was often confusing for both patients and carers when trying to educate themselves about diabetes and learn about their treatment, as the vast majority of literature is aimed at Type I or II diabetes.

Often, in the months leading up to the diagnosis of diabetes, patients with CF will become unwell. They may feel exhausted, become very thirsty, lose weight and present with more chest infections - all due to the high levels of sugar in their blood. It was almost a relief to be able to deliver a definitive diagnosis for these symptoms and to offer some treatment that would undoubtedly help.

Alistair was no exception in that he was extremely unwell, prior to being told he had diabetes. It took a while to diagnose, as he continued to skip clinic appointments and was extremely elusive when we tried to contact him to see how he was. Eventually, he became so unwell that he needed to be admitted to hospital as an emergency - his weight had dropped significantly and his lung function was pitiful. He looked a shadow of his former self and he was weak and fragile.

Instigating the treatment for his diabetes was immensely satisfying. His condition improved almost overnight, following the regular injections of insulin that he required. His blood sugars quickly reduced to an acceptable level, the chest infection subsided and he started to gain weight at an alarming rate.

It was at this stage that Alistair realised we were there to support and help, rather than to chastise him for not doing his treatments and for not coming to appointments. He began to see that there were things that could be done to make him feel better and that perhaps it was worth persevering with treatments after all. A tentative and positive relationship began to flourish between us and he gradually began to take more responsibility for his own health.

Alistair received home visits from us on a regular basis. It was not always easy for him to get to the hospital and it was felt to be important to nurture the vulnerable relationship we had formed. Over the next few years, some of us had noticed that Alistair was beginning to present himself in a more feminine way - dressing in pink, applying mascara and wearing jewellery. None of us commented directly to him, although we did mention it to each other. On one of my visits to his flat, however, he was blatantly wearing women's clothing, including a visible bra. I was torn as to whether I should acknowledge this, and I decided that I should. He had known I was coming to visit and I felt he would not have worn such clothing so openly unless he had wanted it to be noticed.

The floodgates opened - Alistair told me that he wanted to become female. He said that he had never felt comfortable in his own body and he knew he had been born the wrong gender. He had never vocalised this to anyone before, he had not read any information about it and he did not know where he should turn to get some help. His parents knew nothing about these deep-seated feelings and he did not know how they would react. He felt relieved to have spoken about it, but was terrified at the same time.

In the subsequent weeks, Alistair met with our psychologist who in turn referred him to a psychiatrist specialising in gender dysphoria. He talked about the situation with his parents - the hardest conversation he had ever had - and they deserve great credit in how they took the news. The fact that their son wished to change sex was a concept that was completely alien to them. Although such situations are topical and commonplace in today's society, his parents did not follow the news, social media or watch documentaries about such things. His father was a factory worker in a tough, male environment and his mother just could not comprehend how Alistair could feel this way. They found it difficult to adjust and understand, but they did their best and they tried hard to relate to the situation.

Alistair changed her name to Ali and began to live and dress as a woman. It was not an easy time, but she felt relieved that her issues were out in the open and that she no longer needed to hide behind a facade. The team adapted well to the change, but it is extraordinarily hard to remember to call someone by a different name and view someone in a different way, after so many years. I can only imagine what it must have been like for her parents. They could not call her Ali for many months, although they did acknowledge her change in appearance. I remember hearing her father call her Ali for the first time, whilst she was in hospital - it was an emotional moment and Ali sobbed her heart out.

The majority of nurses and other staff on the ward generally accepted Ali's change of appearance and name without any questions. Gradually, over time as new staff began to work on the ward and new members joined the CF team, Ali had never been known by any other name and any issues regarding her appearance or change of gender role became irrelevant. In fact, eventually many of the staff did not realise she had ever been male.

You may wonder why I am telling Ali's story. I want to illustrate how people with CF are just a general cross-section of society in every way. They face challenges, fears and dilemmas just as anyone else would, completely separate from their CF. CF does not define these people; they are people living their lives, who just happen to have CF. I am extremely grateful to Ali's parents for allowing me to share her story.

Whilst Ali was facing these life-changing issues, her CF was still there in the background. In fact, her health was deteriorating fast which made her situation much more complex. She was keen to look into having gender reassignment surgery, but by the time this would have been considered for her, she was too unwell to undergo the surgery. In all probability, she would not have survived the anaesthetic. This was a devastating blow for her and one that she never came to terms with.

For various reasons, Ali was not a suitable candidate for lung transplantation, so as her condition worsened, the options regarding her CF became limited to symptom control and palliative care. She knew that she was dying and she knew we were running out of viable treatments.

There was just one thing she wanted to achieve before she died and that was to have her gender changed on her birth certificate from male to female. I decided that I would do everything I could to help her achieve this goal, but little did I realise how hard it would be and how many bureaucratic hurdles needed to be jumped over before this ambition was realised. Although the procedure was reported to be slightly easier in Scotland than the rest of the UK I, as a relatively literate person, found the paperwork and the jargon totally mind-blowing. I believe that in the last few years, the process has been simplified, but it really was an eye-opening experience for us all. Ali did not have a passport and she did not have a driving licence, both of which are crucial documents to prove identity in these situations. She also required a solicitor for various judicial signatures which she could not afford. She was asked to appear before a court official in person for her own signature to be witnessed, but she was too unwell to leave the flat at this point; nobody seemed to be able to take this on board and waive the rules. After months and months of telephone calls and paperwork, we finally achieved Ali's goal. She received her newly amended birth certificate, stating that her gender was female around two weeks before she died. I was with her when she opened the envelope and she just sank back into her chair and said: *'Now I can die in peace'*.

11
~ Personal adversity ~

When I was in my early twenties, I was diagnosed with asthma. I remember playing squash at the London Hospital sports club and suddenly finding it very difficult to breathe. After several episodes of wheezing, I was finally told that I had mild asthma and that I should start some inhaled medication. I had never needed to take any medication on a regular basis before and I have to admit that I was not good at it. I found it hard to remember my steroid inhaler twice every day and also to carry my 'blue' inhaler around with me in case I needed it.

Over the years, my asthma has been well controlled but every so often I get a flare up of the wheezing, usually as a result of a viral chest infection. When this happens, I often require oral steroids to control the wheezing and to reduce the inflammation - and I think they are miracle drugs for me - within a day I am usually much improved and able to breathe normally again.

Each time I have a severe asthmatic episode, I think of my patients and what many of them they have to go through every day of their lives. Not being able to breathe is unimaginably frightening and is also very tiring. It is like having a ten-ton weight on your chest and having to blow a balloon up through a straw at the same time. Hard work. Last time this happened to me, I couldn't even take a deep breath to sneeze or yawn. I had to sit up in bed to sleep, supported by numerous pillows - not my natural sleeping position at all!

And this is not to mention the pulled stomach muscles caused by too much coughing. Patients would often come to the clinic complaining of muscle strain and rib pain. Sometimes, they would actually have cracked their ribs from coughing too much and this is incredibly painful. In CF, patients are tested for osteoporosis (thinning bones) on a regular basis. This is a complication that some patients get, caused by malabsorption of calcium and certain vitamins, such as vitamin D. For these patients, fractured ribs due to excessive coughing is a real risk - just one more painful and unwanted result of their CF.

For me, having asthma gave me a small and brief glimpse into the lives of those with CF. Most of the time, although I was fine (as long as I remembered my medication) I think that having a condition such as asthma enabled me to have more empathy towards the patients and also gave me some insight into how incredibly hard it is to remember to take your medications every day.

I was generally very healthy and rarely saw my GP. And I was grateful for this, especially when I spent so much of my nursing career looking after others who were not so fortunate. However, one morning in March 2013, I woke up with a strange sensation in my right leg. I had gone to bed the previous night feeling fine, so my immediate thought was that I had slept in an odd position and that things would resolve. A couple of days passed and my leg was not feeling any better. In fact, it was getting worse in that my foot was feeling very numb and I had an uncomfortable feeling of pins and needles all the time. The final straw that prompted me to see the doctor was after I had fed our chickens in the snow one morning. I looked down to see one of my slippers had come off and my foot was so numb that I had not even felt the cold snow beneath it.

The GP was concerned and immediately sent me to the hospital to see the on-call neurologist later that day. I was extremely impressed with the speed of the NHS system - it did reinforce what an extraordinary service it is and how lucky we all are to have it. The neurology registrar happened to be a young doctor who had worked in the respiratory department a year or so earlier. She was an excellent doctor and a good communicator. So important when imparting bad news. Her thoughts (and that of my GP) were that I had Multiple Sclerosis (MS), which is, in fact, a common condition in the north east of Scotland. This obviously had to be confirmed by a few further tests, and I was duly put on the waiting list for these to be done.

This diagnosis was a total bombshell for me. I could not believe it. One day I was just fine and then I am given earth-shattering news in the calmest of ways. Sitting with my husband, Tim, on one side with the doctor on the other side of her desk, she said: *'We think it is MS'*. It must be the same to be told that you have cancer or some other life shortening illness; everything becomes surreal and unreal. Things that were taken for granted just a week earlier suddenly seemed so important and beautiful: like the sunset in the sky as we were driving home, my daughter Emily giving me a kiss, just simply getting out of the car to walk to the front door. I started to look at people in wheelchairs thinking, *'will that be me soon?'*; young people using walking sticks made me question why they needed them. *'Did they have MS too?'*. I looked at my home in a completely different way - it is an old quirky house with uneven floors and steps up and down to several rooms. Should we look at having ramps put in? Would a wheelchair fit through the doorways? Should we look at moving house?

Tim was his usual supportive self, keeping calm and measured but giving me attention when I needed it. The rest of the time he just carried on with life, sorting out the children and getting on with things. That was just what I needed - I did not want sympathy; I wanted things to be normal as they always had been. I felt different, I had been "labelled", but I did not want anyone to treat me differently.

Over the next few weeks, as I waited for lumbar puncture and MRI appointments, my leg got much worse. The numbness and pins and needles spread to both limbs and I was having difficulty walking. It was extremely frightening, but I did not tell many people. I needed to come to terms with it all myself before I could cope with sympathy and concern from others. I only told a few close friends and they were wonderfully supportive to me; I will always be grateful to them. I managed to carry on working, despite having trouble walking any distance. My heart would sink when I was called to the ward - a long walk along several corridors and then up two floors

(I did use the lift) but I was exhausted by the time I got there.

It was at this time I was due to fly to Birmingham to attend the annual UK CF nurse meeting and I had been asked to present the findings of my recent Masters' degree research. My legs were 'giving up on me' day by day and I was nervous and apprehensive about how I was going to manage, but I was determined to get there.

At this point, I want to pay tribute to Lawrie, my colleague and friend from Dundee. I did not know her well at this stage, but I decided she would be the best person to tell about my predicament. She was just amazing. She told me that she would not leave me alone for a minute and would 'look after me' the whole time. She was true to her word! Whenever I looked behind me, she was just there, without being overbearing or making it obvious that she was looking out for me. At the conference she sat right beside me; there she was at the evening meal sitting on my right; when I walked to my hotel room, she was by my side. Even when I was worried about walking to the podium to deliver my lecture, she alleviated my concerns: *'Kairen, I will walk with you to the platform and back to your seat afterwards'*. I don't think Lawrie ever realised how much she helped me over those few days.

By the time I had my MRI and lumbar puncture results, things were slowly improving. This is the way of MS, especially the relapsing and remitting type that they said I had. I cannot fault the hospital staff; they were kind, empathetic and professional. I was given positive information, such as telling me that my 'advanced' age (I was forty-nine!) would probably mean that the MS would be mild and progress slowly. Apparently if someone is diagnosed in their twenty's or thirty's, the disease progression could be significantly worse. I was told that there were a great number of people in the North East of Scotland walking around with mild MS that hardly bothered them at all. There was hope that I would be one of these people. So, I had much to be grateful for: it looked like the condition would be mild and I was very glad it was happening to me and not to one of my children, who were so young and had their whole lives ahead of them.

Even so, I remained sensitive and fragile about the shocking diagnosis and each time I had an appointment with my neurologist, I would become emotional at the very mention of MS. It was at this time that I thought so much of the CF patients - how they must feel every time we delivered devastating news to them, such as a new acquisition of *Mycobacterium abscessus,* reaching the point that we needed to talk about lung transplantation, or a conversation about end of life issues. How dignified and stoical they usually were. I can only remember a handful of times when a patient or their relative started to cry when these things were talked about. Maybe they waited until they got home to have a good sob, or maybe they were so shocked they could show no other emotion at that time. It never ceases to amaze me how incredibly brave people can be in the most adverse of situations.

Following my diagnosis, I was acutely aware of the devastating impact that difficult conversations can have with a patient or family. Breaking bad news is never easy, but some health professionals are better at doing it than others. Everyone will have heard examples of heart-breaking news being delivered in the most insensitive of ways. Medical student and nurse training is certainly getting better in this respect, in that much more emphasis is placed on communication skills early on in training than previously. This can only be a good thing.

For me, nine years on, I am doing well. I have come to terms with my diagnosis and I no longer dwell on what may happen in the future. In these nine years, I have had three acute relapses, all of which have resolved fairly quickly. I am left with a permanently weakened right leg and constant tingling, which does make it difficult to walk any distance without discomfort. However, I have recently bought myself an electric bicycle and I am relishing my regular rides in the countryside, either with other people or on my own. I am finding it incredibly therapeutic, as well as a way in which I can hopefully keep as fit as possible for as long as possible.

This whole period of my life gave me a small insight into what people with chronic conditions must experience every day. It is very different to be a patient rather than a health professional in the hospital. I was very aware of the overpowering 'hospital smell' which I had never noticed in all the years I had worked in that environment; the stomach churning feeling whenever I got a letter stamped with the hospital postmark; marking all the appointments on the calendar; ears pricking up every time I heard 'MS' mentioned on the news or in the papers - it goes on. It is amazing that people can, and do, come to terms with the most devastating news, but the initial impact of diagnosis and effect it can have, should always be uppermost in the minds of those delivering it.

12
~ Should I have a baby? ~

There are many ethical issues and difficult dilemmas when discussing CF, but perhaps none are so emotive or personal than that of fertility and having a baby.

Nearly all men with CF are infertile (rather than sterile) and will be unable to father children naturally. Sperm is made within the testes, but due to a blockage, or total absence, of the vas deferens tubes, they are unable to make their way through the tubes and into the ejaculated fluid. Sexual function in men with CF is normal, but the semen does not contain any sperm. However, around ninety percent of sperm produced in the testes of men with CF is normal, and therefore there are specialist technologies available to enable men to father biological children.

Women with CF are able to have babies naturally and in fact, over the last couple of decades, this is becoming more common. In 2018, sixty-five women with CF had successful pregnancies in the UK, according to the CF Trust Registry. The first reported pregnancy in CF was in 1960 and this mother died six weeks after childbirth. For many years after this, it was considered inadvisable for women with CF to consider having children, but more recently, due to improved longevity and CF treatments, these views have changed. Most UK CF centres may still be cautious in discussing pregnancy in females with CF, but if the woman is well, motivated and has a good support network, there is no reason for her not to have a happy and healthy baby, with minimal effect on her own condition.

Fertility is an area of CF that has always been of interest to me. The ethical aspects of bringing a child into the world, when either parent may have a shortened life or may need to spend long periods in hospital, are areas that need to be carefully considered. For women, the maternal instinct may be incredibly strong and may override rational thoughts about such issues. We always advised our patients that any pregnancy should (if possible) be carefully planned and ideally discussed with the CF team first. Not very romantic for anyone.

The pertinent question of *'will my child have CF?'* is one that must be addressed. It is advisable for the partner to be tested to see if they are a carrier of the CF gene. In the UK, one in every twenty-five people are carriers of the gene. So, if the partner happened to be one of those twenty-five people, there became a fifty percent chance that the baby will have CF. If the more likely scenario occurs (the partner is not a carrier) there is no chance of the baby having CF, although they will definitely be a carrier themselves.

~ ... ~

Careful pregnancy planning did not always happen. I remember one patient, Mandy, who was a challenge for us all - she was young, headstrong and extremely unwell. She was very underweight and on one particular hospital admission, she looked like a frail little bird lying in the bed. She just did not seem to improve on this admission, despite intensive treatment, and one bright spark on the ward suggested the possibility of pregnancy. Although I doubted that she was well enough to become pregnant, the test was done and, guess what, it showed up as positive. It turned out that Mandy was twenty-six weeks pregnant. No one was more surprised than Mandy herself. She was unsure who the father was and was totally unprepared for what was to come.

As a team, we were concerned about the forthcoming months of Mandy's pregnancy. Her CF was severe, she had no permanent home and her support network was negligible. Her mother had abandoned her a long time ago and her father had died a year or so previously. Somehow, she got herself through the pregnancy, spending much of the time in hospital, and she gave birth to a healthy baby boy just a few months later. Without a good family support structure around Mandy, things were always going to be tough. Her baby flourished, but she did not. The whole situation was overwhelming for her and eventually the mother of her best friend took the baby and looked after him for most of the time. Mandy saw him when she could, but this became less and less frequent. She was becoming iller and spent much of her time trying just to live from day to day.

She succumbed to her CF about six months after giving birth. Her little boy was adopted and sadly, we have lost touch with him. I often wonder how he is and what he is doing today. This whole event took its toll on the entire CF team, we had all become very involved with Mandy - it was impossible not to. Her funeral was a tragic affair, with few people attending and, unsurprisingly, her own mother was nowhere to be seen.

~ ... ~

For each heart-breaking situation, we had many more successful pregnancies and beautiful babies born. It was wonderful to see a patient enter into motherhood and realise a long-held dream. Nowadays, many mothers with CF are surviving to see their children grow up and become adults - such different times from even just a couple of decades ago. I was recently asked to give a lecture entitled 'My parent has CF' - a relatively new area in CF and a very welcome development. Our male patients are also increasingly becoming fathers and it is very moving to see someone who was once a belligerent, uncommunicative teenager become a doting and loving father to his precious child.

There remain some health professionals who hold strong views on the ethical aspects of people with CF becoming parents. Without any doubt, the issues involved can be extremely complex and, with the ever-stretched resources in the NHS, there are good arguments to be had on both sides. Should people with a life-limiting condition be encouraged to become parents? Is it moral to bring a child into the world when one of their parents may die early? What about men with CF who cannot father children naturally - should NHS resources be spent on helping them? Should they get priority over others on the waiting list? Should our female patients who are unable to conceive have in-vitro fertilisation (IVF) help? All justified, but difficult questions to answer. And after all, who are we to play 'God'?

The general philosophy in our centre was to allow the patients to make their own decisions, but in a fully informed manner. Our male patients were accepted onto the assisted fertility waiting list, but not at the expense of anyone else - they took their turn like all the other men in the region, who were also desperate to become fathers. Over the years, we did refer two of our female patients to the IVF clinic. Each of these cases were discussed and scrutinised individually with the obstetric teams and decisions were made as they would have been for any other complex situation.

The issues regarding fertility in CF are emotive and personal and there will always be strong feelings on both sides. Many years ago, I remember giving a lecture at a Scottish venue about a case study of one of our male patients, Richard, whose partner had become pregnant with twins following assisted fertility. One of my colleagues spoke up from the audience. He felt strongly that men with CF should not receive help to become fathers as it was unethical to bring a child into the world, knowing that CF would shorten their own lives. I had no idea he felt so strongly about this and was surprised that he was willing to voice his opinions so openly. My own view is that whatever we may feel personally about such issues, it is important to appear open-minded and non-judgemental in front of our patients. Our job is to ensure that patients are able to make their own fully-informed decisions, without any undue influence from us. And then, we should be there to support the patient through their decisions and subsequent outcomes, whether we truly believe them to be the right course of action or not. I am aware that this is often easier said than done, but I do not think an open, honest relationship between the nurse and the patient can exist unless this is the case. I hope that if I gave the same lecture today, twenty years on, the audience would feel unanimously that everyone with CF should be given the chance to become parents in the same way as anybody else.

Incidentally, Richard and his partner lost both twins during pregnancy, it was a tragic time for all concerned. Richard sadly died a year or so after this, but his stored frozen sperm was used by his widow to become pregnant several months later. She now has two beautiful sons and Richard lives on through them both.

~...~

Mary had mild CF. She rarely had chest infections and she came to see us once every three months. She was in her late twenties when she and her husband decided to try for a baby.

She talked to us about her thoughts and plans and we felt she would be a good candidate for pregnancy. We discussed the pros and cons of pregnancy and motherhood, as we did with all our patients and encouraged her to keep as healthy as possible whilst she was trying to conceive. The couple were delighted that the team were happy with their plans and began to start preparing for their future as a family.

Her husband was duly tested to see if he was a carrier of the CF gene and we were all dismayed when his results came back as positive. He was one of the one in twenty-five of the general population who carried one copy of the CF gene. This now meant that there would be a fifty percent chance of the baby having CF for each pregnancy that Mary might have.

What now?

We had many long and detailed conversations with Mary and her husband, looking at various scenarios and options to address them. However, Mary was adamant that she would continue with a pregnancy, regardless of whether her baby was found to have CF or not. She told us many times that she was living a good life with her own CF and who was she to deprive her child of that?

It would have been possible to test her baby for CF in-vitro and then the option of a termination could have been considered if necessary. However, she found this idea offensive. She said that if her parents had had a termination with her, she would not be here today to defend her corner, she would never have lived the life she had led and she would not have had the opportunity to give birth to her own child. We did not try to argue with any of her points. We were there to inform her of the potential scenarios and then to support her decision. One important point for her to consider though, was that although Mary's own CF was relatively mild, this might not be the case for her baby.

Mary did become pregnant fairly quickly and she declined to have her baby tested for CF during pregnancy. Her son, Sam, was born without any complications and he was tested for CF soon after delivery. The results came back a few days later and they were positive.

Sam did have CF.

And so, we had our first mother and son team, both with CF. Mary continued attending our clinic and Sam was seen at the children's clinic. Although it has not always been easy for Mary to juggle her family life, she has coped wonderfully well. Sam is a well-adjusted and lively young man with many interests and plans for the future.

Twenty years on, Sam has transferred over to the adult service. Both he and Mary continue to keep well with their CF, we rarely see them and they lead full and busy lives. Although I have never asked, I am sure Mary would not have done anything differently, given her time again. Her CF is very much a part of who she is and I do not think she would want it any other way.

13
~ To know or not to know? ~

Here is an ethical question: '*If you had a condition for which there was no cure and you had no symptoms, would you wish to know about it in advance?*'.

This can, of course, be applied to many conditions, but in CF it is a question that is regularly asked. CF can range from a mild to severe manifestation of the condition. Some men do not realise they even have CF until they are seen, as adults, at the fertility clinic following the inability to naturally father a child. All men are now routinely tested for CF at the fertility clinic. Imagine being told you are infertile, and *then* that you have CF. There are several men attending our centre who know they have CF, but do not show any obvious symptoms of the condition, except for their infertility.

Since 2003, all babies in Scotland have been tested at birth to see if they have CF. The rest of the UK followed with new-born screening in 2007. For many babies with CF, it is without a doubt, a good thing to be diagnosed at an early stage. Appropriate treatment can begin immediately and the child can be monitored closely. But, for those with *mild* CF, is this a good thing? There has been much debate and discussion over the years about the pros and cons of being diagnosed with CF through the screening process. This is especially pertinent for those with a known mild genotype. There is one particular form of CF which is so mild that it has led to much debate as to whether it should even be known as 'CF' at all. Is it a good thing to be 'labelled' with a potentially life-shortening condition when there are no symptoms? Once a CF diagnosis has been made, the child will become a 'patient', they will be closely monitored for life, with regular hospital appointments, comprehensive annual reviews and a lifetime of possible anxiety with every chest infection or cough. In addition, a diagnosis of CF may affect future job prospects, health insurance status and mortgage applications.

~ ... ~

To bring this to a personal level, over the last year, my own family has had an insight into such an ethical dilemma.

One morning in August 2018, my husband, Tim, woke up with a numb feeling in his left arm and pain in his neck. He is a keen athlete and was a superb runner in his younger days. He has competed in the Grampian Highland Games circuit for the last thirty years, since moving to Scotland, and is a well-known and valued member of the Highland Games light athletics community. The Saturday before he woke up with his numb arm, he had competed in thirteen events at one of the local games - extraordinary for a man of his age. He was extremely strong, very resilient and was never ill.

I have to admit, I was not over-sympathetic initially because I assumed he had pulled a muscle or slept in a peculiar way. However, the numbness in his arm and hand did not subside and eventually he went to see his physiotherapist, who felt he needed an urgent MRI scan. This is always easier said than done within the NHS and Tim did not get the scan until January the following year. In between times, he had been sent for some electrical nerve conductance tests, performed by a neurologist.

Whereas, eight years previously, I'd had a *good* experience of having bad news broken to me, Tim's experience was very different. Following the electrical nerve conductance tests, the neurologist stated in a matter of fact way that he would not be requiring the MRI scan after all. The diagnosis was plain to see, according to his conductance test results. He continued to perform tests on Tim, talking to himself and exclaiming in surprise from time to time: *'I wasn't expecting this!'*.

I tentatively asked him what he was not expecting, feeling uneasy. My intuition was correct - his next words were:

'Well, this is very surprising. What you are able to manage to do with your nerve conductance levels is extraordinary. You have a condition called Chronic Intermittent Peripheral Nerve Demyelination. You will need monthly intravenous infusions of immunoglobulin for the rest of your life. Be thankful there is treatment for this - for most of these conditions, there is no treatment. I'll write down the name of the condition for you as I know you'll 'google' it as soon as you get home. Now, I am sorry - I have overrun as I wasn't expecting to have to do these extra tests with you. My next patient is waiting'.

And with these words, he ushered us from the room.

I was shell-shocked. All I had heard were the words *'demyelination'* and *'monthly intravenous infusions'*. Tim was less perturbed than me, presumably because he is non-medical, and interestingly the words he remembered was that *'there is treatment for this'*. I clutched the scrap of torn paper on which the neurologist had scribbled the diagnosis and sat in the car shaking. I was so angry at the way he had told us the news - he had broken every rule in the book.

We met our eldest son for lunch immediately after this visit and Tim was keen that Will was not told about the bad news. I will never forget sitting in the pub with fish and chips in front of me, acting in a cheerful manner as if everything was fine. In reality, it felt that my world was turning upside down. We must have acted well, as Will never noticed a thing.

Tim did have an MRI scan, despite the neurologist stating this was no longer necessary, and I got a phone call the following week from one of the neurosurgeons, stating that the scan showed severe spinal cord compression from a vertebral disc in the neck, and this would need surgery as soon as possible.

How confusing was this? It turned out that Tim's main issue was the spinal cord compression, causing a weakened and wasted left hand. Because the length of time it had taken to diagnose this, the damage was permanent but we were told that an operation may halt further damage to other limbs. The demyelinating nerve condition was an 'incidental finding' and would not have been found if he had not had the electrical conductance tests.

It was a tough few months. Tim had the operation and recovered well, although it was hard for him to restrain from exercise for three months. However, he was a model patient and it was surprisingly a pleasure for me to look after him. He got back to running as soon as he could and even managed to compete once again in the Highland Games later that summer. Quite remarkable.

The neurology department continued to be intrigued by the incidental finding of the demyelinating nerve condition and argued between themselves as to the actual diagnosis. In the meantime, Tim continued to run and exercise as normal, and did not seem to have any of the symptoms that he was expected to have. At one point, there was even a case conference about him, with both of us present - along with another twenty-seven members of staff, ranging from consultant neurologists and neurosurgeons to medical students. It is not always good to be an 'interesting' patient, although Tim cannot complain that he did not get enough attention from the medical community.

Over a year on, Tim continues to keep well. He does not have trouble walking, he does not have pins and needles and he does not fall over. Apparently, these are all symptoms that he would be expected to have with his condition. He runs two or three times a week and plans to continue competing in the Highland Games until his legs (or some other part of him) give up.

The events of the past year have made me ponder about patients with CF when they get their diagnosis and how they adjust to things. Is it good to know of a mild diagnosis without any symptoms, or is it better not to know?

~ ... ~

Elizabeth was a patient who was diagnosed with CF when she was in her sixties. She had always suffered from chest infections and wheezing, but this was put down to being a sickly child, with asthmatic tendencies. She had been under review at the general chest clinic at the hospital for many years, but nobody had made a link with her symptoms and CF. She was generally fit and well, requiring only the odd hospital admission for a chest infection. She was also overweight (unusual in CF) which probably also contributed to the diagnosis of CF being missed. It was ultimately the diagnosis of one of her nephews with CF that raised alarm bells for Elizabeth. She was duly tested and was found to have a mild form of the condition. Elizabeth had led a full and busy life. She had been twice married and had spent several years living abroad with her second husband. She had three daughters and seven grandchildren. At her current age of seventy-eight, she is probably one of the oldest people in the UK living with CF and she would say that she has lived a great life. We had many conversations about whether it was a good thing that she had been diagnosed late in life with her CF, and she would say without any doubt that she was glad she had not known of her condition sooner. She said that she would not have lived the life she led, she would not have been able to live in Africa and she may not have had her three children. For her, ignorance was most definitely bliss, and she would not have wished things to be any other way.

~ ... ~

The men who were diagnosed with mild CF following tests for infertility issue were usually just seen once a year for an 'annual review'. This was a comprehensive clinic visit that all of the patients attended in the month of their birthday, similar to a car having a yearly MOT. Although most of these men did not have any of the classic CF symptoms, the majority were happy to be seen once a year and it was good for them to get to know us, in case there were issues in the future.

Craig was a patient who was diagnosed with mild CF following a visit to the fertility clinic. He was in his early thirty's and had never had a serious chest infection in his life. He led a full and busy life, was married and had a full-time job as an electrician. He was shocked to hear of his CF diagnosis, despite our assurances that this would be a mild manifestation of the disorder and that we would only need to see him once a year to monitor his condition. He declined our offers of appointments and said he would continue life as normal, without telling anyone about his diagnosis. He did not even tell his wife. This was over twenty years ago and we have not seen him since. I am assuming he still has no CF symptoms, and I often wonder if he ever divulged his diagnosis to anybody.

~ ... ~

To be given an unexpected diagnosis when there are no obvious symptoms is a difficult scenario and one that people will react to in different ways. My husband, Tim, has generally coped well with his diagnosis of demyelinating neuropathy but admits that it has affected him psychologically. The final diagnosis that he has been given is one for which there is no current treatment. He is always alert to any aches and pains that crop up and wonders if they signify the beginning of any worrying symptoms. Most sixty-year old men will get regular twinges and twangs on a daily basis, more so if they are actively running and exercising, as Tim does.

I am not sure what Tim would say if asked whether he would rather have not had this diagnosis. Personally, I would rather not have known about it. Is this being selfish? Burying my head in the sand? I do not know. He has no symptoms, there is no treatment and we do not know what will happen in the future. These thoughts must feel similar for men diagnosed late in life with this mild form of CF, having already been told they are infertile. A double whammy. Is this a good thing? There are pros and cons to this debate and probably no right or wrong answers.

One thing it has taught us is to 'live for the day' because you never know what might happen tomorrow.

14
~ The miracle of transplant ~

Lung transplantation can be a miracle treatment for those with severe lung diseases, including CF. It was probably the most joyous part of my job to see a patient, who had struggled so hard to breathe for such a long time, to be given a new set of lungs. The change is dramatic and immediate. Patients have said that they wake up from the anaesthetic and they feel completely different. They can breathe, they can yawn and they can laugh. What an incredible gift!

The journey to receiving a transplant is often a long and arduous one for most of the patients. There is a severe shortage of lungs for donation in the UK and many people waiting for transplantation do not survive to see new lungs - they die while they are on the waiting list. In recent years, transplant centres have begun to use 'less than perfect' lungs in order to address this situation - lungs from donors who were smokers, drug addicts and so on. If a recipient is happy to receive lungs from such donors (and it is entirely their choice) the likelihood is that they may get their new lungs sooner, although this is not guaranteed.

In the autumn of 2020, Scotland will move to an 'opt in' donor system, where it will be assumed that people wish to donate their organs after death, unless they have stated otherwise. This is something that many people have fought for years to achieve and should, without doubt, provide more organs for donation. However, it should be stipulated that adequate clinical facilities and resources for staffing must also be provided for this to work smoothly for the benefit of patients.

Lung transplantation is a last resort treatment for people with CF and patients are aware that, when we start to talk about this, it is because we are running out of other treatment options. It is always a difficult subject to bring up, as we never know what reaction we may get from patients and their relatives. However, it is often surprising how prepared they are for this conversation, as if it is something they have been waiting for (remember Stuart?).

From the CF team perspective, the timing of such conversations is always difficult. We need to ensure that the patient's condition is declining and their infections are getting harder to treat, but we cannot send them for a transplant assessment too soon either. The wait for new organs can be anything up to two years or more, so we need to gauge how long the patient may have left to live and this is incredibly hard to predict. If left too late for assessment referral, the patient will be refused a transplant as they may be deemed not fit enough to survive the long and difficult operation.

So, it is very important for us to get this 'window of opportunity' absolutely right for each and every patient. There are certain criteria that we use, such as lung function dropping below thirty percent of its predicted value, an increasing number of chest infections, significant weight loss, reduced quality of life and an increased number of hospital admissions. We also use our own judgement and experience to determine the right time to initiate these sensitive conversations. Occasionally, a patient's condition will decline so quickly that there is no time to talk about transplant at all, such as in Anna's case, the patient who was introduced to you in chapter eight; the young girl with *cepacia* syndrome. These scenarios are difficult for everyone concerned, especially the families, who know that their loved ones have missed out on a potentially life-saving treatment. As a team, we always reflected long and hard over such situations to determine whether we should have done anything differently.

The majority of patients referred for transplant will have been gradually declining for several months and will have been suffering more chest infections that have taken longer to recover from. They may have had to reduce their hours at work, or sometimes have had to give up work altogether. They will have started to rely more on family and friends, and everyday tasks that most of us take for granted, will be harder and harder to achieve.

Although the median survival age for someone with CF is improving all the time, many of these patients will be young adults, often in their twenty's or thirty's, relying on others when they should be in the prime of their lives. This adds an extra emotive dimension to the situation; it must be beyond imagination for a parent to see their child dying because they cannot breathe.

Currently, no centre in Scotland offers lung transplantation. The centre that performs the lung transplants for Scotland is in the North East of England. If I needed such an operation, I would choose this centre without any doubt whatsoever. Firstly, their results are amongst the best world-wide. The care and treatment there are superb and I cannot praise the staff more highly. Due to the complex and long-term nature of the patient's conditions, I got to know the transplant co-ordinators and consultants well over the years and I never ceased to be impressed by their caring attitude and in-depth knowledge about each patient. I spent some time working with them at the centre on a couple of occasions and what a job they have. I would not like to be in their position - when a pair of lungs becomes available, they know there will be several deserving and suitable patients, desperately needing them, many of whom may have been on the waiting list for a significant length of time. How do you choose who gets them? They will, of course, have strict criteria to follow but they will often end up needing to choose between two or three patients, all of whom they will know well. This must be such a difficult decision to make and one that I do not envy.

For the patients, the wait for a lung transplant can be excruciating. They will know that their condition is so bad that transplant is the only option left to them. But they do not know *when* that call for the operation will come. They are advised to be ready at all times, with a bag packed, because when lungs do become available, they will only have a short time to prepare to leave. From our corner of Scotland, the patients need to take an air ambulance plane, which is met by a road ambulance to carry them to the transplant centre. Ideally, they need to be at the centre within three to four hours of the initial phone call. One stipulation is that a carer should accompany them on this journey, which means that they also need to be on 'standby' for the call. Their place of work needs to be informed, holidays may need to be cancelled and day-to-day plans may be disrupted; but all for a very good cause.

Unfortunately, the awaited call may take many months. Or, as is common, there may be several 'false alarm' calls. Many patients are told that lungs are available for them and they travel all the way to the transplant centre, to be told that the donor organs: *are not good enough*. Or the patient themselves may have had a raised temperature or other signs of infection on arrival, meaning that it would be too risky for the operation to go ahead. If this is the case, the patient and their carer usually have to make the long journey back to Scotland on the train (or in a road ambulance if very unwell). Imagine the feeling of disappointment and deflation as you are travelling back home without new lungs. It certainly can be a difficult time.

All the while a patient is on the waiting list, their condition will be deteriorating. This is hard for the patient and their family. There is a light at the end of the very long tunnel, but how do they ensure that they will reach that light? With each chest infection, the lungs will be a little more damaged and the patient may be perceived as being less and less able to withstand a major operation. At some point, the move from active treatment to palliative care may need to be made. CF is so different from other conditions, where it is usually easier and more straightforward to determine when end of life care should begin. With the possibility of a transplant ahead and the chance of the miracle that this might bring, it is sometimes impossible to take this hope away. I have seen and heard of many cases in CF where active treatment continues up until the patient's death; intravenous antibiotics and physiotherapy are still administered until the very last minute. The rights and wrongs of this can be debated endlessly, as with so many aspects of CF treatment, but each situation must be taken individually and the best treatment must be given for the patient at that particular time.

~...~

Alana was a headstrong and feisty patient in her mid-thirties. She'd had a hard time over the years as her mother had left the family when Alana was in her teens and, more recently, her father had left the North East of Scotland to move to England with his new wife. Alana had a sister living locally, with whom she had lost touch due to a falling out, and she had another sister living in London. She also had a brother who had been in prison for several years. She had a close circle of friends but no relatives that she could rely on nearby. She was a tough cookie in that she'd had to fend for herself for a number of years, despite her deteriorating CF. She had lurched from job to job, either losing her position due to taking time off or because it became harder for her to get to work on public transport. She was one of those resilient people who 'just got on with things', even in the most adverse of situations and I always admired her tenacity. I remember her being probably the most uncommunicative and grumpy teenager I have ever met - her attitude towards us and her CF was scathing and scornful and I did not see her smile for several years! Twenty years on, we joke between us what a nightmare she was and she apologises on a regular basis. I was very touched to read in the retirement card she wrote to me:

'I don't even know where to begin or how to express my gratitude for all your hard work, care, love and affection over the years ... even when I was a "shy" pain in the ass. I don't know how you put up with me! Ha ha'.

During 2017, Alana went significantly downhill in terms of her CF. This sometimes happens, for no particular reason - it is often just due to the lungs becoming so damaged with infection over the years that they start to become useless. Breathing becomes more of a struggle, infections become more intense and harder to treat, and just day-to-day living becomes a mountain to climb. Alana was needing to spend more and more time in hospital and she eventually had to give up work completely. She continued to live independently in her small council flat and she relied totally on benefits. But she also relied on the team. We became her surrogate family, as she did not have anyone else. And because of this, we became very close to her and got to know her extremely well.

She had been urgently referred for transplant assessment and had been placed on the active waiting list in the summer of 2017. Her father and sister had both come up from the south of England to spend time with her and to accompany her to the assessment centre. She struggled through the next few months, mostly on intravenous antibiotics in hospital. But in December she suffered a worse chest infection than usual. Her condition was deteriorating rapidly and we were in close touch with the transplant centre about her condition. We knew that lung transplantation was her last option and that it needed to happen quickly.

One morning I arrived at work, and Alana had been moved through to the intensive care unit. She needed one-to-one care and the nurse looking after her appeared extremely concerned. Alana was suffering badly, she was struggling to breathe despite high flow oxygen, and her blood gas figures were dire. She was also extremely frightened and did not want to be left on her own. The medical staff were conferring between themselves about discontinuing active treatment and moving to palliation (meaning commencing medication, such as morphine, to allow her to die peacefully). We called her father and sister and informed them that the situation was not looking good for Alana and asked them to come urgently to be with her.

We had maintained close communications with the transplant centre over the last few days so they were fully aware of Alana's condition. After much deliberation at their end, they asked us whether we thought she would manage an air ambulance journey to down them? They were keen to have her down there in case lungs became available for her. She would be under their noses and they would know exactly how robust she was should the time come. Alana's condition was stabilised as much as possible and an air ambulance was booked. She was accompanied on her journey by a multitude of tubes and machines as well as an intensive care doctor and nurse. She arrived at the centre two hours later - fragile, weak and vulnerable, but still alive and with her fighting spirit, which had never left her.

It was another twenty-four hours before suitable lungs became available for Alana. However, yet another blow was dealt when she was told the organs were too damaged and were not good enough to use. She had no choice but to wait a bit longer. It seemed as if everything was conspiring against her. But, finally, less than a day later, a further set of lungs were in line for Alana. As before, everyone scurried about setting everything in place for the operation, like a well-oiled machine. And on this occasion Alana did receive new lungs. She survived the operation and woke up from the anaesthetic breathing new life into them with every inhalation. What a miracle. And what an incredible example of the NHS functioning at its best - working as one team between two different centres, and indeed between two different countries.

Alana returned to Scotland six weeks after her transplant. She could not wait to see the team and her first visit to the clinic was a sight to see. She made such an effort: her make-up was perfect, her outfit was stunning and she wore a pair of stiletto heels! She made quite a statement as she waltzed down the corridor as only she could. To see someone looking so bold and self-assured when she had been so close to death just a few weeks before was very humbling. It was just wonderful and was one of the best days of my nursing career.

~ ... ~

When a patient does get the call for transplant, it is an exciting time for all concerned. These calls may often happen at the weekend or late at night, so the CF team may not always hear about them until the next day, when the operation may have been underway for several hours. The operation is usually long and arduous - CF lungs are often very damaged and can be stuck to the sides of the chest wall, which makes them difficult to remove. It is always a relief for everybody to hear that the procedure has been successful and the patient is on their way to the intensive care unit. The long and stressful wait for the relatives will take its toll; they must feel so helpless at these times, knowing they can do nothing but wait. Usually their wait is rewarded, as the difference in someone as soon as they wake from the anaesthetic is immediate and palpable.

Successful lung transplantation is an extraordinary treatment for those with CF, when all other options are running out. However, embarking on the transplant journey is not straightforward; it is a rollercoaster ride of ups and downs, of the unknown and of an uncertain future. It takes strength, bravery and resilience of body and mind to withstand all the obstacles that get in the way and the hurdles that have to be jumped. It does, without a doubt, help that the majority of CF patients who undergo transplantation are young and relatively resilient, in that their hearts and other organs will usually be strong.

It is, however, the psychological aspects of transplant that can be so difficult to cope with. Usually, the resilient nature of those with CF seems to get patients through this difficult time, but one aspect that I always found interesting, following a successful transplant, was the 'grieving' for the previously ill person that is no longer there. For so long, the patient (and their carers) will have devoted their time and effort into keeping as well as possible; the immense burden of treatment, hospital admissions, close and frequent links to the CF team, and generally receiving intense care and attention almost twenty-four hours per day. Most patients do move on and begin to function as a 'well' person relatively quickly, but there are some who find it much harder. There may also be a feeling of guilt that someone else has had to die for the lungs to become available - this is fairly common and one or two patients that I have looked after have required intensive psychological input over this period to come to terms with the situation. Recipients are told a few details about their donor, such as sex, age range and type of death. If the recipient wishes, they may write to the donor family, expressing their gratitude and this will be passed to the family, via the transplant co-ordinator. It is known that donor families will often gain much comfort from receiving a letter of gratitude from the recipient, whose life has been saved by a decision made at a time of great adversity. Occasionally, a correspondence has been established between the recipient and the donor family and this can be rewarding for both parties.

When successful, lung transplantation can be a remarkable treatment for people with CF, who are reaching the end of their lives due to their damaged lungs. In our centre, one patient is now over seventeen years post-transplant, his lung function remains at ninety-seven percent of its predicted value and he is now in his late fifties. Quite amazing. Long-term data for survival post-transplant is improving all the time and it may be that more lungs will be available after autumn 2020 when the 'opt-out' system comes into place. I will always remain in awe of the dedicated transplant team and co-ordinators who work so hard to enable these incredible, lifesaving procedures. And of course, the most gratitude should go to the donors and their families, whose selfless acts in allowing their organs to be used, makes the whole process possible.

15
~ Mia's story ~

You have already met Mia in chapter six. Mia was the young girl who had moved to Australia, but returned to the UK for her wedding in the fairy-tale castle in the Scottish Glens. That was several years ago - Mia went back to Australia following her wedding and has lived and worked there ever since. I have seen her from time to time when she comes back to see her family, but months can go by, with only email contact.

Over the last couple of years, Mia's CF began to deteriorate and she was placed on the lung transplant list in early 2019. She received her hew lungs in August 2019 and after a roller coaster ride, she is now doing extremely well and is making the most of every minute!

She has kindly agreed to write her story for you - it means so much more to hear personal experiences first-hand and I am extremely grateful to her for allowing me to use her own words in this book.

My transplant journey

The beginning of my transplant journey was so special, filled with much emotion, shock, fear and also a huge realisation that either way my struggle was over, truly there was something immensely calming about this. The phone rang at midnight on Saturday 25th August, when I was sound asleep. I woke up so fast when I heard the transplant nurse's voice. The process had begun: "start fasting, we will phone back in 2 hours as lungs are just being checked, you'll need to be in hospital by 6am". I hung up the phone and my partner and I burst into tears. I couldn't stop grieving for the family that were literally standing by their loved one's bed, struggling to come to terms with such loss. Yet, in their most tragic time, they were about to give me the gift of life. The tears flowed and flowed and still to this day, it is a moment in time I will never be able to truly describe. The tears still flow when I think about it. On 25th August 2019, I was the luckiest person alive to get a second chance and I vowed I would do everything to honour my donor. I was no longer "I" because for the next 24 hours, I became "we". I received what can only be described as medical science at its' best and a true miracle. No words will ever capture the gratitude and happiness that I felt.

Coming out of the operation itself and being on the ventilator was OK and not as bad as I thought. I was heavily medicated on pain relief with epidurals, long and slow acting opiate pain relief and a million transplant medications. I was awake and speaking within 10 hours of actual surgery and on my feet doing my first walk within 24 hours (walk is a bit of a stretch - I shuffled, ha ha).

On day four, the epidural was removed and I have never felt pain like it. I felt like something out of "Game of Thrones"! I couldn't lift or pull a thing, couldn't use my arms to get out of bed, had to be fully supported and be *lifted from the centre of my back. I had huge internal bruising, a broken sternum, which was wired back together, severe burning nerve damage across my chest (showering was murder!), I could no longer feel underneath my breasts, my actual nipples were excruciating. I had numbing down my right arm and left glute, at certain times of day I couldn't tolerate loud sounds. The muscle mass and weight as my body went into full recovery plummeted off me. I couldn't walk down stairs without my legs giving way or shaking like mad. I had four drains in my chest, which to be fair, were the size of "garden hoses" and I am not joking! I then had a family of "chicken feet" lines hanging from my neck, and arterial line in, oxygen on, nebulisers, cannulas in my arm, a bladder catheter in and just to top it off beautifully, a million bruises everywhere from insulin, blood thinning injections, finger pricks and a mountain of reflux too! I felt like a vice was wrapped around me so couldn't get a deep breath at all. Seriously, I had never looked or felt so good – ha ha!*

The road to recovery was long and hard, and only once began once I left hospital. Side effects from the anti-rejection drugs, fungal medications, anti-viral treatments and everything else started to build up in my system, causing unwanted problems. I was overwhelmed by the amount of medication, memory loss (this really impacted me), no confidence to look after myself, all these new side effects - and I had no idea which were normal and which were not. Throughout the transplant process, everyone will get their own set of complications, not everyone gets everything and some recipients suffer far more than others. For me, my side effects included A2 rejection within the first month, minor collapsed lung, shaking, severe muscle spasms, slight bleeding of the brain, became diabetic type 1 (drug induced), and kidneys not functioning very well. I needed an MRI scan of the brain to rule out epilepsy or a stroke, as one day I was admitted to the Emergency Department as I couldn't talk properly and was shaking violently. It turned out that I had toxic levels of one of the rejection drugs in my body. I had night sweats, terrible chills right to the bone, even in 30-degree Australian summer heat. One day, I ended up doubled over on the ground because my period, for some reason, gave me two months of excruciating pain. Sometimes, I'd have a period three times in a month. My diabetes became an absolute nightmare to manage, and at times I couldn't help thinking "what have I done?", only to burst into tears with guilt, as I remembered that someone had given me the gift of life. It was the biggest rollercoaster of emotions one could ever imagine, one minute you are facing Death, after years of suffering - to survival, to euphoric joy, indescribable pain, gratitude beyond words, to the dark days when once again, you would lose your fight. I have experienced it all, I'd break down to random nurses at times, it truly became all too much at times but somewhere inside me, a fire was still lit. Giving up was never an option and I didn't care if I shuffled through that day, it was another step forward and the light at the end of the tunnel started to shine so brightly.

The journey is worth EVERY HARDSHIP YOU WILL GO THROUGH!!

For me, the Sun Rose Again ... for anyone else waiting for a lung transplant, IF I COULD GIVE YOU A DAY IN THE LIFE OF BREATHING ONCE YOU ARE RECOVERED, it would take all your fears away. Stay Strong, IT WILL GET EASIER. Shuffle, shuffle, cry, swear, laugh, tell everyone your story and feel it all. You WILL come through it.

At around six months, I really started to feel more myself, medication was being adjusted to the right level, pain was so much better, I was back exercising 4-5 times a week, I was back at work and the energy I had was just insane! I no longer suffered chronic fatigue, I got to socialise again, the colour of pink returned to my nails (instead of blue), my skin became so clear and the whites of my eyes were so bright. I could not believe how healthy I looked - I had no idea how sick I was until I experienced the other side of "normal lungs".

I can lie on my back and just breathe.

I don't cough, no more yucky mucus, my breath is endless and when I do fitness classes, my muscles give up before my lungs – ha ha! For the first time in ages I had hope, I had a future and I have never felt so much happiness - and I mean real happiness, that is indescribable.

The day I packed away my nebuliser and CF drugs was so much fun! No more oxygen, feeding machines or nebs at the side of my bed, just a lovely book and lamp.

Oh, so simple, but it brought me such big smiles. I started to really plan, booking events and concerts again, horse riding competitions, fitness classes. I was like a Duracell battery. I am so grateful for the tiniest things, such as getting up and putting a washing load on, without struggling. Eating, talking and showering without even thinking about how out of breath and drained I would be. Walking and talking at the same time - I had no idea such a thing was possible! To appreciate the level of suffering I had made me realise what indescribable joy and gratitude feels like.

Another sunset or sunrise sends me beaming with smiles, simple walks down the beach and grabbing that coffee without even thinking about it.

Every day is an absolute blessing and I stretch out every hour to squeeze in as much as I can - to be honest I cannot keep up with my donor lungs!

16
~ Death and Dying ~

It is hard to move on from the positivity of lung transplantation and Mia's story to the issue of death and dying, but as much as transplantation was a significant part of my job in CF, so sadly was the process of dying, in cases where transplant was not a viable option or when it was unsuccessful.

Although there have been many advances in the world of CF, the premature death of our patients is still too common. CF is such a complex condition and despite the fact that treatments have greatly improved, especially over the last decade or so, there is still some way to go before the condition can be 'cured'. Fortunately, death in childhood due to CF is extremely rare nowadays and longevity is increasing all the time. However, most of the deaths I experienced during my years in CF were with young people and this can be incredibly hard. It definitely seems the 'wrong way round' - for a parent to see their child dying. There is no word in the English language to describe a bereaved parent, and yet we are all aware of the words 'widow', 'widower' and 'orphan'.

In my years of working in CF, I experienced numerous deaths, all of which were painful, poignant and tragic. Each one affected me in a different way and I always said to myself that the moment they ceased to move me was the time to give up working in this field. This never happened; I feel I was as emotionally involved with patients on the last day of my working life as I was on the first day.

Death in CF is nearly always due to respiratory failure, which occurs when the lungs just do not work anymore. It gets harder to breathe and infection eventually can take over, causing irrevocable damage. The oxygen and carbon dioxide levels in the brain become unbalanced and this leads to drowsiness, confusion and eventual coma.

Other organs may become affected, such as the kidneys and liver, and finally the body will begin to shut down. This can either be a fairly long, drawn out process, or things can move quickly and a more rapid death may occur. Although the latter can possibly be easier for the patient, in that they do not need to suffer the prolonged process of dying, it can be harder for the relatives as it gives less time to prepare and to say their goodbyes. Much research has shown that if relatives or carers have had time to be able to prepare for death, the grieving process will be less traumatic for them. A sudden and unexpected death is difficult for all concerned, for obvious reasons.

Palliative and end of life care is an area of medicine that has made significant advances over the last few decades. It is no longer such a taboo subject as it once was, and this field is now recognised as being as important as other specialities, such as cardiology or orthopaedics. There are now multidisciplinary teams in palliative care, based both in acute hospitals and in hospices, and expertise in this area is developing all the time.

I chose to do my Masters' degree in 'Enhanced Palliative Care' - a subject that has only been on offer for the last few years. My thesis was a research project asking CF Specialist Nurses throughout the UK about their experiences in talking to patients about death and end of life issues. I had a phenomenal response from my nursing colleagues. Long and emotional pieces were written about recent experiences of death, or indeed deaths from years before, which had scarred and left their indelible mark on the CF teams. Without exception, end of life conversations were considered difficult, but necessary, talks to have with patients and relatives. However, in reality, it was felt that they could often have been handled better and, in some cases, the conversations never happened at all. In my research, it appeared not to matter how long the nurse specialist had been in post for, or how many years of experience they may have had, this conversation did not get any easier. All respondents said they felt they needed further training in this area, but that it was difficult to find the time and resources to do this.

Whilst all health professionals acknowledge that end of life conversations are difficult, the question should be asked for *whom* are they difficult? I would argue that one of the reasons these conversations may never happen is because it is too painful for the health professional themselves. They may not want to cause hurt and anxiety for the patient or their relatives; they may not know how to instigate the conversation; they may be unsure of which words to use or which facts to divulge. Whereas, in fact, it has been shown that often patients and relatives are waiting for the subject to be raised by a health professional and are often relieved when it happens. In one research study, although around three quarters of patients said they would feel comfortable talking to their doctor about end of life issues, in reality only a quarter of patients said their physician actually raised the subject spontaneously.

I recall one incident, having just given a talk in our department entitled 'How to have a Good Death', one of the consultants came up to me afterwards and confessed that he felt unable to discuss death and dying issues with his patients. He acknowledged that this was a serious fault of his, but that he just could not do it. It was brave of him to admit it to me, but surely it was an aspect of his daily work that should be urgently addressed?

~ ... ~

Joe was a young patient who was studying politics at university. He was an interesting person, in that he was a deep thinker with a dry sense of humour and was obviously highly intelligent. Throughout his childhood and adolescence, he had managed his CF well with the help of his parents, but at university, things started to go downhill. We often had young people with CF who moved to our centre when they started at university in the city and it was not unusual for their CF to become worse, at least initially. It was hard to leave home, move into halls with a crowd of other students and balance the work/play lifestyle that is unique to university life. Health was often neglected and medications forgotten. All very normal behaviour, but with tough consequences when you have CF.

Often, this downward trend in health can be reversed, but this did not happen in Joe's case. He became more and more unwell and needed to spend long periods of time in hospital. His studies suffered and although his university tutors were trying their hardest to help, this was a cause of great stress to him. Over the next few months, things did not improve and as a team, we were seriously concerned for his long-term outlook. Although Joe would talk to us about anything else, he would not discuss his health or his deteriorating condition. We tried to instigate the conversation many times and also gave him every opportunity to talk about how he felt about dying, but he shut us out every time. He would not discuss transplantation with us and he appeared unable to address the fact that his health situation was getting serious. The CF psychologist became involved, but she struck the same barriers as the rest of the team. He did not appear to be depressed or distressed, in that he was still able to joke with us and he continued to be sociable with his friends. I assumed that he was using denial as a way of coping with the earth-shattering and momentous events that were unfolding before him. In other words, burying his head deeply in the sand.

As time went on, it was becoming clear that Joe was reaching the end of his life. He was deemed unsuitable for transplantation for various reasons, including his low weight, so we began to discuss the issue of palliation. However, until the day he died, he would not discuss any aspect of his health with the team, his parents or his friends. This was a source of great consternation to us as a team and his parents, and we all spent many hours discussing it amongst ourselves. How could we have managed things better? I even presented his case at a national CF meeting after he died, to ask a wider audience for their thoughts. One wise voice spoke up and asked: *'who were we concerned for?'*. We had obviously tried to raise the issue with Joe, we had given him every chance to discuss it, had he wanted to. We had done our 'bit' and it was Joe's choice whether he wished to engage or not. Were we feeling we had failed because he hadn't wanted to address his mortality? He said that as long as we offered patients the opportunity to talk, it was then up to them what they did with that information. Joe was an intelligent person and there was a high chance that he had taken in everything we had been trying to say, but had chosen not to discuss it with us further. This was his prerogative and we should respect that. How right the audience member was, as you will see later.

~...~

Joe's death was a long and drawn out process, as happens with many of the patients. It is hard for all to watch this happening, especially if the person is in distress or frightened. There are many excellent medications available now to alleviate symptoms, but the *fear* of dying is a more challenging aspect to address. It is important for everyone to be open and honest about what is happening, so the patient does not feel that anything is being hidden from them. If they do want to talk about how they are feeling, it is vital that they are given time and space to do this. There may be some concerns that can be addressed at the time and this will alleviate anxiety, such as *'who will look after my dog when I am gone?'* or *'I am worried about my finances'*.

The UK charity, the CF Trust, has recently produced an excellent publication[2] for documenting end of life wishes specifically for young people with CF. This is a non-threatening, comprehensive booklet covering many issues, including documenting particular thoughts and concerns before death, passwords for devices and social media and wishes for funerals. In the last year or so, we have been using this document with patients well before they are at the end of life stage of their disease and this has been accepted positively by everyone. There is no pressure when or where to complete it and, having discussed it with the patient first, we often leave it with them to complete in their own time. If the patient prefers, we will sit with them and we can fill it in together. This process can generate conversation and the patient may

---

[2] Advance Care Planning for People with Cystic Fibrosis, CF Trust 2017. https://www.cysticfibrosis.org.uk/life-with-cystic-fibrosis/planning-for-end-of-life

also feel more comfortable in raising concerns and anxieties, which they may have not done otherwise.

~ ... ~

I clearly remember one young patient who died unexpectedly, about three hours after we had completed this document. As it turned out, it was so fortunate this had been done before he died. For various reasons, there had been much friction between his partner and his family, who lived a few hundred miles away, and there was some heated debate about where he should be buried. He had clearly stated in the document, just before dying, that he wished to be buried near his home in the south-west of Scotland, so that his mother could visit his grave on a regular basis. At such a traumatic and stressful time, it was good to be able to resolve this dispute by expressing his direct wishes, and they were duly followed - he was buried near his childhood home and his mother is able to visit him every day, which means the world to her.

~ ... ~

Where a patient would like to die is an important issue to address and this is also covered in the CF Trust document. This may change depending on at what stage the patient is at and how they feel at various times. One patient, who was nearing the end of his life, documented that he would like to die at home but changed his mind a few weeks on, saying he would prefer to die in hospital. He felt he would rather be surrounded by staff who knew him and who had expertise in alleviating his symptoms, rather than being at home with his elderly mother, who may have felt out of her depth and very alone. In my experience, the majority of patients did die in the respiratory ward in the hospital, a handful died in their own homes and only one or two in the local hospice. The main reason for this, I believe, is because the ward was familiar to the patient, they were well known to the staff, the CF team were close at hand and if they were on the lung transplant list, active treatment could be continued, as necessary, by staff who knew them well.

For those who chose to die at home, the CF nurses and other team members would offer as much support as necessary and also involve the community services, such as district nurses. The CF nursing team would do everything possible to be able to spend as much time with the patient and family at home, and I hope it would have been of some comfort to them to know that we were there. It was also often cathartic for us to be there, as saying goodbye to a young person with whom we'd had so much involvement over the years could be very painful for us too.

To be with a patient at the very end of their lives is a precious and privileged place to be, whether in the hospital or at home. I consider myself fortunate to have been able to be with some of the patients during the last few hours of their lives, but there have been some more traumatic patient deaths where events have happened too quickly for any of the CF team to be involved. As soon as we are born, the one thing that is certain in our lives is that we will also die. Women will often have detailed and lengthy childbirth plans, where they request as natural an event as possible, but this does not always happen - although I wished for a natural, drug-free birth with my eldest son, I ended up with an epidural and emergency section after a long and painful labour. The same will apply to death - how ever we may hope to die and even if our wishes are carefully documented, this may not occur in reality. In the years that I worked in CF, two patients died in road traffic accidents and two others died suddenly of issues that were non-CF related. There were also a number of patients who had sudden deaths with haemoptysis (coughing up blood). Haemoptysis is not uncommon in CF, where the blood vessels in the lungs can become enlarged and engorged. Sometimes these vessels will burst, causing extensive bleeding, occasionally leading to death. These traumatic deaths are much harder for relatives and carers to deal with - there is often no time to plan or prepare, or to say goodbye.

The death of a young person, in whatever circumstances, is always a tragic, poignant and sad situation. It is such a waste of life and what could have been is left unknown. There is nothing to be said or done that will bring that person back, but by just 'being there' at a time of such grief can be a source of great comfort to those left behind.

We used to continue to visit families for as long as they wished to still have contact with us. For some, this was for several months, for others it was only for a short time. I remember one mother did not want to see me at all following her daughter's death, she said she wanted to forget the CF and remember her daughter for other things instead.

I have witnessed many young deaths in my nursing career, but even so, I remain unable to even begin to imagine the pain and grief that a parent goes through at this time. Everyone copes in their own way when they have experienced the death of someone close to them and there is no right or wrong way to behave or feel. People will have bad days and those that are not so bad; gradually the 'not so bad' days become more frequent and glimpses of light may be seen through the darkness. The adage that 'time is a great healer' is probably correct, but it is often hard for many bereaved people to be able to look ahead to see when such a time may occur. Small things may trigger feelings of despair and anxiety - I remember one mother, who felt she was having a 'good day', telling me that she just dissolved into tears at the freezer section of a supermarket when she saw the frozen peas; these had been her son's favourite vegetable. Another mother could no longer watch 'Pointless' on TV as this had been the time when she and her son had sat together each afternoon to enjoy the programme.

Very, very gradually, and in their own time, most people will start to come to terms with the death of their loved one and they will learn to live a new way of life. For some, this will take longer than others and there will always be certain times of the year when they may feel they are back to square one, such as birthdays and anniversaries. For others, who have spent so much of their time caring for the person with CF, a whole new way of life will be required. Previously, hours were spent each day concentrating on physiotherapy and medications and when that person was no longer there, huge gaps in the day would appear, with long periods of emptiness, that needed to be filled. We were able to provide counselling sessions for those who felt they needed it, through various CF charities, which was a great source of help to many.

This was such a difficult time and I was always filled with admiration at the stoical and dignified way that so many people managed to cope with this momentous event that had occurred in their lives. Even those whom I thought would never be able to laugh or smile again do manage eventually. It has never ceased to be unbelievably humbling to me to witness human nature at its strongest.

17
~ Jenna's story ~

When lung transplantation is successful, it is the most miraculous of treatments, especially for people with CF. When it does not go well, it can be totally heart-breaking for everyone involved. For the second time in their lives, patients will be facing their own mortality. This time, it is much worse as they will have been given a glimpse of normality after their transplant. They will have had some time being able to breathe normally, to be able to walk without oxygen and they will have been able to laugh without convulsing into a coughing fit. When it all goes wrong after transplant, it is tragic for all concerned.

This happened on a handful of occasions during my years in CF and each time was a situation that I will never forget. Those involved will have already known what it was like to have been near death - the period before their transplant will have been the toughest time for them, not being able to breathe, constant chest infections, hospital admissions, no appetite and the huge burden of never-ending medications. They will have suffered the psychological effects of not knowing what the future will hold for them, if they may become too unwell to have the operation or if they may die before lungs become available.

Then, the call comes from the transplant centre! New lungs are donated and the person will experience a new lease of life. The euphoria felt during this time is incredible. To be able to talk, laugh, yawn and sneeze without coughing and choking, things that most of us take for granted and do every day without thinking. Jenna told me of the day she walked across the road shortly after her transplant and was able to carry home a bag containing two bottles of lemonade - this was such a major achievement for her and she was so delighted to be able to manage it.

So, let me tell you more about Jenna. She was a young lady in her early twenty's when she had her transplant. She'd had the usual route to transplant - becoming progressively more unwell over the previous few years, until she was desperately ill and struggled to get through every day. She lived with her parents and two younger siblings and they were a close family. Jenna was a spiritual person, she thought and felt deeply about all sorts of things and was mature beyond her years. She bore her illness with grace and dignity and everyone was overjoyed when she finally got her transplant.

The weeks following her operation went according to plan and Jenna started to enjoy the reality of living her life again. Although she still needed to take a multitude of medications and her other CF related complications remained present, she was able to breathe!! I remember she came to the clinic one day and was waxing lyrically on what it was like to have a 'normal' cold. She was sniffing and sneezing and most people would probably be complaining about feeling a little unwell, but Jenna was so excited that it had *not* gone into her chest, as would have happened before. She said she had never had a head cold before like other people, and she was enjoying every minute of it!

It was wonderful to see Jenna well again. She was embracing life; she was keen to return to work and she was socialising with all her friends once more. She even went abroad for a family holiday. During this time, she had continued to be seen on a regular basis at the transplant centre and they were delighted with her progress.

But it was not to last. Six months on from her operation, Jenna started to feel breathless once more. She was seen at the transplant centre for a routine check and her lung function had dropped significantly. She underwent a bronchoscopy and acute rejection was found to be the cause of her sudden onset of breathlessness. Episodes of acute rejection are relatively common post-transplant and occur when the immune system tries to attack the new lungs after recognising that the new organs are 'foreign' to the rest of the body. This acute rejection is usually treated, with good effect, by increasing medication, such as steroids and immunosuppressive therapies.

However, there are other types of rejection that can arise, which are more serious and harder to treat. It soon became apparent that Jenna's form of rejection was this type, known as bronchiolitis obliterans syndrome. Although this can be treated successfully for some people, Jenna did not respond to treatment and her condition rapidly went downhill. This was heart-breaking to witness - to see someone embracing a second chance at life and to have this taken away from her was cruel beyond words. There was nothing to say, no words that could take away the fact that this was so unfair. Jenna had been given a glimpse of normality, a short chance to re-engage with friends and work, but just as she was getting used to this, it was all taken away from her.

It was not long before Jenna was bed-bound for the second time, due to breathlessness and failing lungs. And then, there came a point where there was no further active treatment that we could give her. The transplant centre said that they could not offer her a second transplant; there were so many other people on the waiting list at the time, who had not had a first chance of this treatment. The heart-rending conversation with her and her family about moving to palliative treatment was one of the hardest I have been involved in. She wished to die at home and everyone did everything possible to enable this to happen. She had a beautiful bedroom - I remember it so well, it was ethereal and tranquil with curtains that floated at the window and mobiles that chimed quietly in the breeze. It was peaceful and Jenna was not scared. She told me that she was ready to die, she had tried her best and could not fight any more. She said she was not afraid of dying, there had to be a better life beyond this and although she was not religious, she knew she would see her family again.

To be genuinely unafraid of dying is one of the most generous gifts anyone can give to those left behind. It can be of immense comfort to those who have been bereaved to know that their loved one had faced their death with courage and strength. I have seen many people die in this way, including my own father, and I have also seen those who have been terrified. It is hard to watch someone who is frightened of dying; relatives have told me that they are haunted by those final images for a long time afterwards. Nobody knows in advance how they will cope with their own deaths, but I am always amazed at how many do seem to approach this time with acceptance and dignity. A good death is something that we all strive to achieve and I do believe that Jenna's death was as 'good' as any of us could have hoped for under such incredibly sad circumstances.

Jenna was a remarkable person and I know she is someone who is still remembered with love and admiration by everybody who knew her.

18
~ The final goodbyes ~

In all cultures and religions, a funeral is an important part of someone's death. Archaeologists have found evidence of funerals dating back to over three hundred thousand years and funeral customs have been said to consist of five 'anchors', which are: symbols of significance, gathered family and friends, rituals, culture and either burying or cremating the dead body. In some countries, the funeral is seen as a celebration of life and in others it will be a more sombre affair. There are countless traditions, rituals and customs connected with funerals but the basic premise is to give everyone a chance to say 'goodbye' to the person they knew, surrounded by other family and friends. I have attended all sorts of funerals, from religious ceremonies, to humanist funerals and 'green' burials - all have been a beautiful and fitting tribute to the person who has died.

In the western world, people often document their wishes for their own funerals nowadays, using advanced care directives, and this can be cathartic for the bereaved relatives when planning the funeral; to know they are carrying out the desires of their loved one. I have attended funerals where people have been asked to wear colourful clothing, or a bit of tartan or even funny hats. Beautiful music has been played at the request of the person who has died or sometimes humorous songs that sum up the person perfectly. One young patient, Bruce, was a passionate Celtic supporter and demanded that he was buried in his Celtic football kit. He also asked for the Celtic anthem to be played during the funeral, so imagine everyone's astonishment when the dulcet tones of the Rangers anthem rang out to all in the crematorium! I looked over nervously to Bruce's mother sitting in the front row who looked quite horrified. The poor person who had made this momentous error quickly rectified the situation and the correct anthem was played to our great relief. The long outward breath was audible in the room. Bruce's mother was very magnanimous about the whole debacle afterwards and said how amused he would have been about the mistake.

I am not so sure.

~ ... ~

I want to return to Joe, the young politics student, who was unable to discuss his mortality with us. We had assumed that he was either in complete denial or was totally unaware of his situation. After he died, his mother found a letter he had written to her and his father, which included a list of stipulations that they should follow after his death. It was long and detailed and was written by someone who had been totally in control of his feelings and wishes.

He had planned his funeral to the last detail, including asking to be buried in a wicker coffin. He wanted his university chaplain to conduct the service and he stated which music he would like to have played. These were standard requests, but then came the ones that were more difficult to fulfil. Joe had written that he did not want his parents to attend his funeral. He wrote that parents should never be expected to be at their own children's funerals and he would not want to put them through this pain. Another request he made was that he should be buried in the back garden of the family home.

His parents were just amazing. It is not easy to have been left a letter from your son, asking you to accommodate his wishes following death, especially when two of them were not easy to follow. The standard requests were not a problem - Joe did have a wicker coffin, his funeral was conducted by the university chaplain and the music played at the ceremony was as he had asked. But for his parents not to attend the funeral? They had to be there. The service would be incredibly painful for them, as for any parents, but they had to be there. I remember his mother saying: *'This might make you cross, but I am sorry Joe, we will be there to say goodbye to you - there is nothing you can do about it'*. And, it was the most beautiful funeral - one they could not have missed for the world.

They then had to face Joe's next request: to be buried in the back garden. His parents researched at length the possibility of achieving this wish and although it is not illegal, in reality it would have been an almost impossible task to do. It would also mean that it would have been very difficult for his parents to ever move on from this house for sentimental reasons, and in addition, who would buy it knowing there was a body buried in the garden? There were also many legal hurdles to jump over, which made it extremely hard for his parents to comply with this wish. However, they did not give up and eventually managed to resolve this dilemma - I had immense respect and admiration for them and their perseverance, especially at a time of such sadness and grief. They bought a corner of land from the farmer who owned the field behind their house and once they had obtained the necessary council licences, Joe was buried beside his family home. The corner of land was an idyllic spot, with an abundance of wild flowers and woodland nearby. It could not be more perfect and I know that Joe would have been proud of his parents for enabling this wish to be fulfilled.

~ ... ~

In 2008 there was a spate of five deaths within nine months at our CF centre. This was a traumatic and difficult time for everyone, including other patients and the entire CF team. Four of the deaths had been young people and they had all known each other well. It was hard to attend their funerals so close together, within the space of a few months (one of which had been Bruce's, the Celtic football fan). The following year, the team psychologist suggested that we should have a Gathering of Remembrance for the families of these patients. The hospital chaplain became involved and managed to secure us a strip of woodland to use for this purpose, at one of the local National Trust castles nearby. We will always be grateful to the National Trust for allowing us to use this piece of woodland. It was a little off the beaten track and the views were stunning. We purchased a wooden bench and my colleague suggested the perfect words of *'Take a breath here'* which were duly inscribed onto it.

Almost fifty people attended the ceremony which was non-religious, despite being led by the chaplain. It was cold, wet and windy but it did not dampen the spirit of the day and it was a beautiful and meaningful event. After the ceremony, I was chatting with Bruce's grandmother and I will never forget her words: *'That was beautiful, and what lovely words written on that bench ... "take your **last** breath here" ...'.* I just managed to nod and agree with her.

We held the Gathering of Remembrance again ten years later, after we'd had another bad year with several deaths within twelve months. This time, the sun shone and a violinist joined us, who played beautifully haunting music in the woodland. Many relatives who had come to the first gathering returned for this one and it was very moving to see how they were able to speak to and comfort those who had been more recently bereaved.

There are many ways to remember and celebrate the lives of those who have gone; some will be more personal (sitting on the bench beside Joe in his magical woodland) and others will be more public such as the Gatherings of Remembrance. Each and every person will have their own ways of reflecting on the lives of their loved ones and it should never be forgotten that human nature is strong and resilient. Somehow, people usually do get through these momentous and life changing events to begin to smile and laugh again once more.

19
~ The future is bright ~

The last few chapters were difficult to write, I found them emotional and nostalgic, bringing back so many poignant memories for me. So, now we have got to the final chapter of the book and I want to end on a positive note. Because, there is so much to be positive about in the world of CF.

When I started in my CF career in 1993, people with CF were dying too young. Over a quarter of a century later, death is still coming too soon for some, but many others are living longer and healthier lives. In 1993, there were twenty-four patients attending the clinic and now, as I have reached my retirement, we have over seventy patients at our centre. The children's clinic was much bigger than the adult centre in the early 1990's - now the adult centre is more than double the size of the paediatric clinic. It has been said that those born today with CF will be expected to have a near normal lifespan. How remarkable is that? Some adult centres in the UK are getting too big and are having to restrict the number of patients they can see - this would have been unheard of twenty years ago. So, there is much to celebrate in the field of CF and those with the condition should be feeling positive and hopeful about the future.

The reasons for more people living long into adulthood with CF are multifold, probably mainly due to improved treatments, especially developments in antibiotic therapy. As the pernicious bacteria, so commonly found in CF lungs, have become more resistant and harder to treat, it became imperative that other medications were developed to treat the condition.

Over the last decade or so, some incredible new drugs have come onto the market to treat CF. Whether you have CF or are involved in caring for anyone with CF, whether you know someone with CF or whether CF has never touched your life personally, I am sure you will have seen something in the press about these new medications. The main issue is the cost, something that in an ideal world should never enter into healthcare - but sadly this is not the case. It is hard for CF to compete with all the other demands on the health service.

These medicines are called cystic fibrosis transmembrane conductance regulator modulators (CFTR modulators) and I'm afraid I cannot begin to explain in detail how they work. Put simply, the CFTR modulator drugs target the faulty proteins within the cells and work to control their effects by moving them to the cell surface and helping them function properly. In other words, they 'switch off' the fault in the cells, to allow them to work again. I am in awe of the research scientists who have designed these extraordinary medications.

In chapter one, I mentioned it was important to know the CF genetic mutation for each patient. This is because different CFTR modulator drugs will work for different mutations and it is vital to be prescribed the correct medication that will work for each specific mutation. The first of these targeted drugs became available in 2012 and were designed to work for a relatively rare mutation, affecting approximately four percent of patients with CF in the UK. Interestingly, this particular mutation (G551D) is much more common in Scotland, affecting around twelve percent of the CF population.

We had a number of patients with the G551D mutation and we prescribed this drug for them as soon as we were able. The change in their condition was miraculous for many of them. And the change happened almost immediately. Patients felt better, coughed less, and their weight and lung function increased. I remember one of our patients exclaimed: *"shut the f****ing front door!!!"* when she saw how high her lung function was, just a few weeks after starting this drug. I had never heard that expression before.

At the time of writing this book, a further CFTR modulator drug has been developed and is being marketed aimed at those with only one Delta F508 mutation. This medication will be effective for around ninety-eight percent of people with CF in the UK - almost the entire CF population. Initial research results for this medication are very encouraging and there is cause for great optimism for the future of people with CF.

There is a big 'but' though ... the cost of these drugs is astronomical which has made it prohibitive for most health authorities to fund on the NHS. I am not going to enter into the politics of the reasons for this high price tag, but it has been an incredibly frustrating time for the CF community and it has been extremely divisive. The knowledge that these magical new drugs, which could transform quality of life for so many with CF, are available, but that they are out of reach due to the cost. It is like having a tasty carrot dangled in front of you, which you are never quite able to reach.

The CF community is a powerful lobby and there has been much publicity about this issue. I have no doubt that the latest CFTR modulator to be marketed will eventually become available to all of those who fit the criteria - the results appear so good that it would be unethical not to allow this to happen. We will wait to see what happens with baited breath.

I believe that we are entering into the most exciting period in CF that I have seen in my career. Who knows what the next decade will bring? Without any doubt, a cure for CF is potentially within sight. At the last CF conference I attended, I mentioned to a colleague that I felt sad to be retiring at such an exciting time, but he wisely said to me: *'Why be sad about that? Far better to be retiring at an exciting time rather than a time of doom and gloom!'*. How right he was ... and I will not be actually 'leaving' the world of CF; I will always be involved, even if from afar, and I will be watching every new development from the side-lines with hope and expectation.

For those who have died before having access to these incredible developments in CF: you will never be forgotten and your strength and stoicism will live on through your families and those who knew you.

~...~

As I look back on my career in CF, I consider myself so fortunate to have worked amongst the most incredible group of people - patients, families and colleagues. I never knew what challenges and opportunities each day would bring - life was never boring for one single moment in this job. Some days were beyond exhausting, both physically and mentally. There were some situations that were heart-breaking and harrowing and other days that were unbelievably uplifting and joyous. There were the usual stresses and strains of working within the NHS, with all the unrealistic demands and pressures put on staff to perform, but there was also the chance to see the mechanics of the NHS working at their best. How teams will pull together at times of clinical urgency and how resources can be found when absolutely necessary to provide the best possible care for patients is an extraordinary accomplishment. It truly is a wonderful institution, for all its faults, and we all have good reason to be incredibly proud of the NHS and its staff.

CF remains a complex condition which poses a daily challenge for all those who suffer from it. The patients that I have known over the years have been a source of great inspiration and education to me. They have taught me how to live life to the fullest, how to enjoy every day and how to conquer adversity. They have shown me how to cope with the toughest challenges that life can throw at you with humour and strength. Collectively, they are an uplifting and motivating group and many of them have never ceased to amaze me with their resilience, motivation and positive attitudes.

It has been a pleasure and a privilege to have played a part in caring for them and their CF. This book is dedicated to all of the patients I have known over the years and I want to say a heartfelt thank you to every one of them.

Addendum

Since this book was completed, there have been some further developments regarding CFTR Modulator drugs.

On 30th June 2020, NHS England agreed a deal for the triple therapy medication with the company currently manufacturing this drug. This was followed by similar deals in Wales on 22 July 2020, in Northern Ireland on 30 July 2020 and in Scotland on 4 August 2020.

This is exciting news for those who are eligible for this medicine.

Acknowledgements

There are so many people to thank for their part in this book that it is difficult to know where to begin.

But of course, my heartfelt gratitude goes to all of the patients and their families with whom I have worked in the world of Cystic Fibrosis. Their strength and resilience through the roller coaster ride that is CF is like nothing I have encountered before and they have taught me about the things that really matter in life. They truly are an inspirational group of people.

Without my colleagues over the years, I would not have been the nurse I became. Thank you to all the inspirational people I have encountered throughout my nursing career: Jackie Applebee, Clive Andrews, Harriet Spencer, Theresa Bathelmy, Denise Patnell-Fiddy, Debby Madden, Hilary Hignell, Ken Earle, Paul Cullinan, Adrian Evans, Liz Whelan, Carolyn Rogers, Veronique Bataille, Julia Newton, Bee Squire, Bertie Squire, Adrian Taylor, George Bird, Elizabeth Friend, Ruth and Jon

Dowell, Pat Hoddinott, Moira Dale, Lynne Wolfe and many, many others.

Throughout my CF career, I have met countless people who have devoted much of their career to work in this field and I have learnt so much from all of them: firstly, thank you to all my CF MDT colleagues throughout the years: James Friend, Joe Legge, Owen Dempsey, Prasima Srivastava, Graham Devereux, Elsie Thomson, Isobel Yackiminie, Margaret MacLeod, Jen Still, Alison Copeland, Steph Cruikshank, Susan Mackay, Caroline Sommerville, Kathy Kindness, Gordon MacGregor, Lawrie MacDougall, Lynne McIntosh, Aileen Mallinson, Amanda McGrath, Richard Brooker, Jane Young, Susan Hempsey, Lesley Blaikie, Gill Brady, Mags Pogson, Helen Rogers, Sam Philip, Shirley English, Vhairi Bateman, Douglas Fraser-Pitt, Deborah O'Neill, Tricia Ferguson, Claire McCullough, Tessa Williamson and so many more - you know who you are.

A special mention to my wonderful CF nursing colleagues: Sandra Steele and Genna Wood. We had such fun times throughout the trials and tribulations of the job and I miss working with you both.

The nurses who work so hard on the respiratory ward, helping to care for the CF patients - we could not have done our job without you and I know it was challenging at times. Your dedication and patience are things you should all be very proud of.

I also want to mention two special friends who, although are non-medical, they have always listened to the ups and downs of my job with empathy and compassion. They were both so encouraging to me during the writing of this book – thank you, Nicola and Hilary.

The support and help I received for this book from Jane Grieve and Julia Banfield was hugely appreciated. Thank you both, for spending time and effort in reading the draft copies and for all your positive and constructive feedback. Your wisdom and knowledge were invaluable.

And finally, thank you to my family: my parents, my husband and my three beautiful children. I would not have been able to do any of this without you.

About the author

Kairen Griffiths began her State Registered Nurse training at The London Hospital in Whitechapel in January 1980. After working for several years in the east end of London, she moved to the north-east of Scotland and trained as a District Nurse. She gained a degree in nursing from Robert Gordon's University in 1995 and she obtained a Masters' degree in Enhanced Palliative Care from the University of Stirling in 2010. She began looking after adults with Cystic Fibrosis in 1993 and spent the next twenty-six years devoting her career to this special group of patients. In March 2019 she won the British Journal of Nursing runner-up award for the 'UK Nurse of the Year' in London. She retired in September 2019. She lives in Scotland with her husband and has three grown up children.

To contact the author:
kaireng@aol.com

Further copies of this book can be obtained at:
www.lulu.com

9781716677748

Lightning Source UK Ltd.
Milton Keynes UK
UKHW020632171120
373555UK00011B/709